# Establishing a Project Management Foundation

## Using Microsoft Office Project 2003

Gary L. Chefetz

Dale A. Howard

# Establishing a Project Management Foundation
Using Microsoft Office Project 2003

Copyright © 2004 Soho Corp. dba MSProjectExperts

Publisher: Soho Corp.
Authors: Gary L. Chefetz, Dale A. Howard
Cover Design: Tony Valenzuela
Cover Photo: Peter Hurley

ISBN 0-9759828-5-0

Library of Congress Control Number:  2004097518

Published and distributed by Soho Corp. dba MSProjectExperts, 398 Valley Road, Gillette, NJ 07933 (908) 626-1404 http://www.msprojectexperts.com

## EPM Learning

EPM Learning is a complete series of role-based training manuals for professional trainers and corporate training programs. To learn more about the EPM Learning courseware series for Technical Administrators, PMO Administrators, Project Managers, Resource Managers, Executives and Team Members, or to obtain instructor companion products and materials, contact Soho Corp. by phone (908) 626-1404 or by email info@msprojectexperts.com.

# Contents

Contents

*Contents*

# About the Authors

**Gary Chefetz** is the founder and President of the Soho Corp. and msProjectExperts, which exist to support businesses and organizations that choose the Microsoft enterprise project management platform. Gary has worked with Microsoft Project since 1995 and has supported Microsoft Project users since the introduction of Project Central in early 2000. Gary continues to receive the prestigious Microsoft Project Most Valuable Professional (MVP) award for his contributions. As a long-time MVP, he works closely with the Microsoft Project product team and support organizations. Gary is dedicated to supporting Microsoft Project Server implementations through his business efforts with clients and through his contributions in the newsgroups. Contact Gary Chefetz online in one of the Microsoft Project newsgroups at msnews.microsoft.com or e-mail him at:

gary_chefetz@msprojectexperts.com

**Dale Howard** is an enterprise project management trainer/consultant and is Vice President of Educational Services of msProjectExperts. Dale is a Certified Technical Trainer (CTT) who has more than 11 years of experience training and consulting in productivity software. He has worked with Microsoft Project since 1997 and volunteers many hours each week answering user questions in the various Microsoft Project communities. Dale received the prestigious Microsoft Project Most Valuable Professional (MVP) award in 2004 for his expertise with the software and for his contributions to the user communities. Dale is married to Mickey and lives in Denver, Colorado. Contact Dale online in one of the Microsoft Project newsgroups at msnews.microsoft.com or e-mail him at:

dale_howard@msprojectexperts.com

# Introduction

Thank your for reading Establishing a Project Management Foundation Using Microsoft Office Project 2003. Herein find a complete learning guide and reference to managing projects using the Microsoft Project desktop application. Our goal in writing this book is to teach you how to use Microsoft Project effectively as both a desktop project management tool and enterprise project management tool.

We take a systematic approach to the topical ordering in this book beginning with an overview of the project management process, followed by two modules that provide an overview of Microsoft Project features and functionality. The succeeding nine modules demonstrate how to use Microsoft Project properly during each phase of the project management process. Module 04 shows you how to define a project, while Modules 05, 06, and 07 teach you how to plan project tasks, resources, and assignments. Modules 08 and 09 show you how to baseline a project, to enter actuals into the project plan, and to track project variance. Modules 10 and 11 deal with plan revision and change control issues, while Module 12 teaches you how to print project Views and Reports.

Throughout each module, you get a generous amount of Notes, Warnings, and Best Practices. Notes call your attention to important additional information about a subject. Warnings help you to avoid the most common problems experienced by others and Best Practices provide tips for using the tool based on our field experience.

Because you have read this book, we believe that you will be much more effective using Microsoft Office Project 2003. If you have questions about the book or are interested in our professional services, please contact us at our office. If you have questions about Microsoft Project or Project Server, contact us through the Microsoft public news groups.

Gary L. Chefetz, Microsoft Project MVP

Dale A. Howard, Microsoft Project MVP

msProjectExperts

# Module 01

## Project Management Overview

### *Learning Objectives*

In this module, we will review:

- The PMI definition of a project
- The project management process according to PMI

# Project Management Theory

What is a Project? According to the Project Management Institute (PMI), a project is "a temporary endeavor undertaken to create a unique product or service." (PMBOK, 2000) According to the PMI definition, a project is:

- Temporary – Every project has a definite beginning and a definite end.
- Unique – Every project is something that your organization has not done before, and is, therefore, unique.

# The Project Management Process

Because Microsoft Project 2003 is a project management tool, you will use the software most effectively in the context of the normal project management process. Therefore, it is important to become acquainted with each of the phases of the project management process, and with the activities that take place during each phase. According to the Project Management Institute, the project management process consists of five phases: Definition, Planning, Execution, Control, and Closure.

## *Definition*

The Definition phase of a project authorizes the project, and is a part of the project's scope management process. The Definition phase of a project usually includes the creation of one or more Definition documents, such as:

*Project Charter* – Chartering is a process that produces a document recognizing the existence of a project. The Project Charter includes the following aspects:

- The product or service description
- An analysis of the business need
- The authority to assign resources to the project.

Developed by senior management and stakeholders, the Project Charter feeds the development of the Statement of Work document.

*Statement of Work* – The Statement of Work (SOW) document defines the project and the product or service produced by the project. The SOW can include one or more of the following sections:

- Executive Summary
- Phases, Deliverables, and Activities (Tasks)
- Sponsor Responsibilities (Rules of Engagement)
- Assumptions and History
- Acceptance Criteria
- Change Control Policies and Procedures

Other names for a Statement of Work document are a Proposal, a Business Plan, a Scope of Work, or a Scoping Document.

*Work Breakdown Structure* – A Work Breakdown Structure (WBS) document breaks the work on a project into meaningful components. The WBS includes project phases, deliverables, and task. You can see the WBS in the Task Sheet portion of any project in Microsoft Project 2003.

## Planning

The Planning phase of any project is of major importance to its potential success. According to the PMBOK, the Planning phase of a project can include any of the following processes:

- Scope Planning and Definition
- Activity Definition
- Activity Sequencing
- Activity Duration and Work Estimating
- Resource Planning
- Schedule Development
- Cost Planning and Budgeting
- Risk Management Planning
- Project Plan Development

## Execution

The Execution phase of a project is the process of moving forward with the project by performing the activities associated with the project. Execution also involves coordinating the resources to carry out the project plan. Execution includes each of the following processes:

- *Saving a Project Baseline* – Prior to beginning work on the project, you must save a baseline for your project. You will use the baseline to compare project progress with initial project estimates and to analyze project variance. You should save the project baseline at the beginning of the project, and you should never change the original project baseline.

- *Tracking Project Progress* – Collecting actual project data is critical to the success of the project. You should gather actual progress from your project team on a weekly basis.

- *Analyzing Project Variance* – Throughout the life of the project, you must analyze project variance and trends, and look for trouble spots in the project plan in an effort to make informed decisions about revising the project plan.

- *Revising the Project Plan* – Based on the results of variance analysis, you may need to make minor revisions to the project to realign all aspects of the project to stay within its predefined scope, schedule, and budget.

- *Reporting Project Progress* –Throughout the life of the project, you should seek to identify the informational needs of project participants, and create reports to meet these needs.

## Control

During the Execution phase of the project, you must maintain control of the project to ensure that your project meets its objectives. Some of the common aspects of project Control are the following:

- *Change Control* –Change Control is the process of managing changes to the predefined scope of the project.

- *Continued Communication* –A critical component of controlling any project is communication. You must keep communication lines open at all times with all project participants.

## Closure

The Closure phase of the project formalizes the acceptance of the project and formally closes the project. Project Closure can include any of the following aspects:

- *Project Closure Methodologies* – Clearly defining "Exit Criteria" is critical to the success of a project.

- *Lessons Learned* –It is a wise practice to evaluate the completed project and to compile the lessons learned for use in planning future projects.

- *Template Creation* – Successful projects lead to template creation for similar project types. It is part of your job as a project manager to define project types, build templates to meet project types, and to modify templates to meet the unique needs of each project.

# Module 02

# Microsoft Project 2003 Overview

## *Learning Objectives*

After completing this module, you will be able to:

- Understand the purpose of the Global.mpt file in Microsoft Project 2003
- Understand how to use the Getting Started task pane
- Effectively use Help
- Understand the features of the Microsoft Project 2003 user interface
- Use navigation tricks to navigate more easily in the Microsoft Project 2003 environment

# Introducing the Global.mpt File

Microsoft Project 2003 uses the Global.mpt file as the template to create all new project files. The Global.mpt file is very similar to the Normal.dot template that Microsoft Word uses to create all new word processing documents. When you launch Microsoft Project 2003, the software opens the Global.mpt file into memory. You can use the Global.mpt file to store project customization that you would like to be available for use with any project, such as custom Views, Tables, Filters, Groups, Reports, etc.

 When using Microsoft Project Professional 2003 with Project Server, the software opens an Enterprise Global file into memory, in addition to your Global.mpt file. Organizations can use the Enterprise Global to distribute enterprise customization such as Views, Tables, Filters, Groups, Reports, and Macros to all users quickly and easily.

# The Startup Task Pane

By default, Microsoft Project 2003 displays the Getting Started task pane to the left of the Gantt Chart each time you open the software, as shown in Figure 2-1. Task panes provide a common area for commands that require more information than a toolbar button can provide. You can use the Getting Started task pane to connect to the Office Online Web site, to open existing projects, or to create a new project.

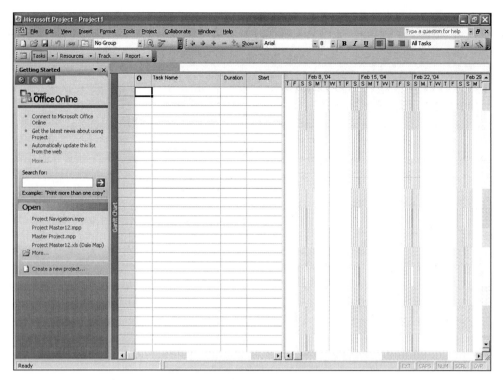

**Figure 2-1: Getting Started
task pane**

You can access additional task panes in the Getting started task pane by clicking the down arrow on the Getting Started header. The other task panes are:

- Search Results

- Help

- New Project

- Shared Workspace (enterprise only)

Figure 2-2, 2-3, and 2-4 show the Search Results, Help, and New Project task panes.

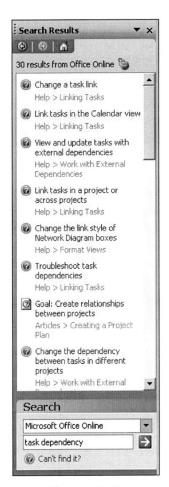

**Figure 2-2:**
**Search Results**
**Task Pane**

**Figure 2-3:**
**Project Help**
**Task Pane**

**Figure 2-4:**
**New Project**
**Task Pane**

You can close any of the task panes by clicking the Close button (the X button) in the upper right corner of the task pane.

 To turn off the automatic display of the Getting Started task pane, complete the following steps:

1. Click Tools ➢ Options and then select the General tab

2. Deselect the Show Startup task pane option and click the OK button

When you close any of the task panes, Microsoft Project 2003 automatically displays the Project Guide sidepane, which is one of the Help features of the software.

# Microsoft Project Help

Two useful Help features of Microsoft Project 2003 are the following:

- The Project Guide
- The Planning Wizard

## *The Project Guide*

The Project Guide in Microsoft Project 2003 assists you with using the software during every step of the project management life cycle. The Project Guide consists of two parts: the Project Guide toolbar and the Project Guide sidepane. The software displays both of these Project Guide features when you start Microsoft Project 2003. Figure 2-5 shows the Project Guide toolbar.

**Figure 2-5: Project Guide Goal Bar**

The four named buttons on the toolbar (Tasks, Resources, Track, and Report) assist you with task planning, resource planning, tracking project progress, and reporting on a project. The software displays the assistance in the sidepane. The first button on the toolbar (Show/Hide Project Guide) allows you to display or hide the sidepane temporarily. Each button also contains a drop down arrow that you can use to display a list of all help topics for that button. Figure 2-6 displays the help topics available for Task planning.

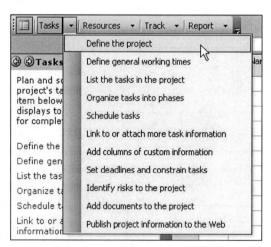

**Figure 2-6: Project Guide help topics for task planning**

Figures 2-7 and 2-8 show the Project Guide sidepane.

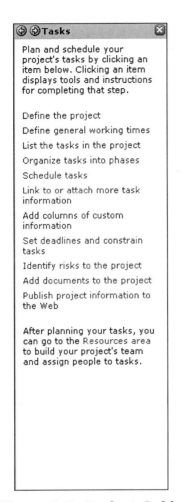

Figure 2-7: Project Guide
sidepane for Tasks

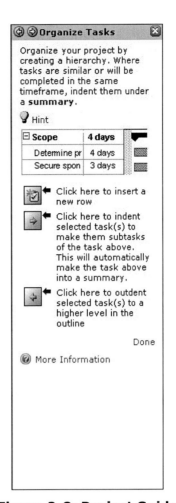

Figure 2-8: Project Guide
sidepane to Organize Tasks

To use the Project Guide sidepane, click one of the four topical buttons on the Project Guide toolbar, and then click any of the topics displayed in the sidepane. Once you have selected a topic, the software displays additional steps for that topic in the sidepane.

To find additional help on any topic in the Project Guide sidepane, click the More Information hyperlink at the bottom of the topic window. When you are finished with a topic, click the Done button.

 Your organization can customize the content of the Project Guide to match your project management methodologies and procedures. To do so requires knowledge of XML, HTML, DHTML, and Microsoft Project 2003 VBA programming.

If you do not want to use the Project Guide sidepane and toolbar, complete the following steps:

1. Click Tools ➢ Options and then select the Interface tab
2. Deselect the Display Project Guide option, and then click the OK button

## *The Planning Wizard*

The Planning Wizard is an interactive Help feature of Microsoft Project 2003 that gives you advice as you work on your project. The Planning Wizard's advice falls into three categories:

- Advice about using Microsoft Project
- Advice about scheduling
- Advice about errors

The software displays the Planning Wizard any time you take an action that will cause it to activate in any of the above three topics. For example, setting a Finish No Later Than constraint on a successor task displays the Planning Wizard message about scheduling shown in Figure 2-9.

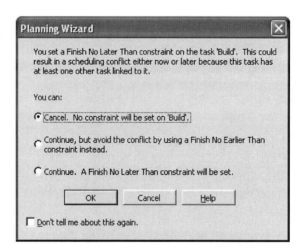

**Figure 2-9: Planning Wizard
message about scheduling**

You can control the function of the Planning Wizard through several settings in the project Options dialog box. To display the Options dialog box, click the Tools menu, click Options, and click the General tab. Figure 2-10 shows the Planning Wizard options.

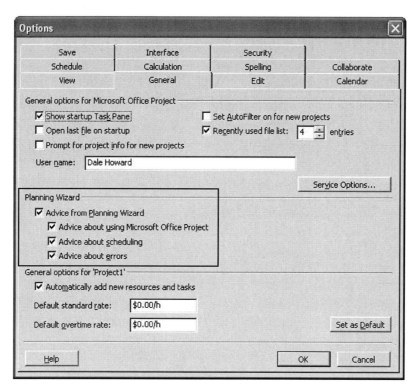

**Figure 2-10: Options dialog, General page**
**Planning Wizard options**

 If you select the Don't tell me about this again option in any Planning Wizard dialog box, you will disable a part of one of the Planning Wizard options shown in Figure 2-10. To turn on a disabled option, display the project Options dialog box, and then select the desired option.

# Navigating in Microsoft Project 2003

To become familiar with Microsoft Project 2003, it is wise to know the names of the some of the common objects in the user interface. Figure 2-11 labels many of these common objects.

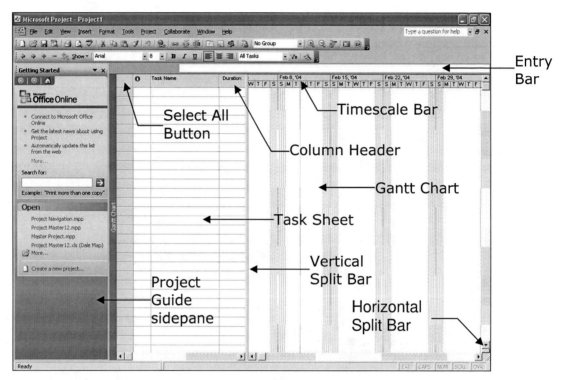

**Figure 2-11: Microsoft Project 2003
User Interface with Labels**

 By default, Microsoft Project 2003 displays adaptive menus, with the Standard and Formatting toolbars on the same row. The adaptive menus feature allows you to see only the most recently used items on each menu. Showing the two toolbars on the same row reduces the vertical space used for toolbars. If you find these two features frustrating, you can disable them by completing the following steps:

1. Click Tools ➢ Customize ➢ Toolbars

2. Select the Options tab

3. Select the Show Standard and Formatting toolbars on two rows option

4. Select the Always show full menus option and click the Close button

## Use the Scroll Bars

Drag the scroll box on the vertical scroll bar to scroll to exact Task IDs and Task Names.

Drag the scroll box on the horizontal scroll bar to scroll to precise dates in any task view.

## Use the Zoom In and Zoom Out buttons

The Zoom In and Zoom Out buttons on the Standard Toolbar adjust the timescale for viewing specific timeframes of schedule detail.

 You can set a custom zoom level by clicking View ➢ Zoom. In the Zoom dialog, select your desired level of zoom and click the OK button.

## Use the Go to Selected Task button

Click the Go to Selected Task button on the Standard Toolbar to bring the left edge of the Gantt bar into view for the selected task.

## Screen and Tool Tips

Microsoft Project 2003 offers you many helpful screen tips and tool tips that you can display simply by floating your mouse pointer over an object in the user interface. For example, Figure 2-12 shows the date screen tip when you hover the mouse pointer over the Timescale bar.

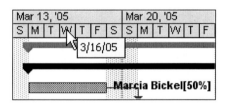

**Figure 2-12: Screen Tip
on Timescale Bar**

 You can see other useful screen tips and tool tips when you float the mouse pointer over the Select All button, column headers, Gantt bars, and link lines between dependent tasks.

# The Three-Tiered Timescale Bar

The three-tiered Timescale Bar allows you to display a different time unit on each tier of the Timescale Bar. The default setting of the Timescale Bar shows only two tiers formatted with Weeks on the top tier and Days on the bottom tier. Each tier of the Timescale Bar shows the time units displayed in the Gantt chart at the current level of Zoom. To add a third tier to the Timescale Bar, complete the following steps:

1. Double-click anywhere on the Timescale Bar to open the Timescale dialog shown in Figure 2-13

2. Click the Top Tier tab

3. Click the Show drop-down list in the Timescale Options section and select Three Tiers (Top, Middle, Bottom)

4. Select your desired time Units and Label in the Top Tier Formatting section

5. Click the OK button when finished

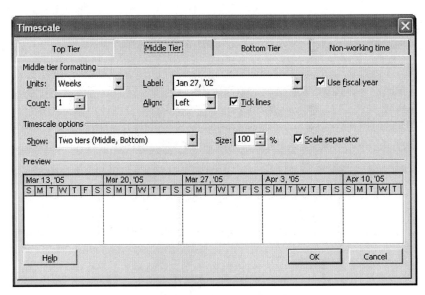

**Figure 2-13: Timescale Dialog Box**
**Top Tier Page Selected**

If your company uses a fiscal year different from the calendar year, you can use the three-tiered Timescale bar to display the fiscal year against the calendar year. To do so, complete these steps:

1. Click Tools ➢ Options and then select the Calendar tab

2. Select the beginning month for your fiscal year in the Fiscal year starts in drop down list and click the OK button

3. Double-click the Timescale bar

4. On the Top Tier page, set the Units to Year, and select the Use fiscal year option

5. On the Middle Tier and Bottom Tier pages, deselect the Use fiscal year option and click the OK button

Figure 2-14 shows the three-tiered Timescale bar set to display the fiscal on the top tier against the calendar year on the middle and bottom tiers. Notice that the fiscal year begins on April 1.

|  | 2005 |  |  |  |
|---|---|---|---|---|
| Qtr 1, 2004 | Qtr 2, 2004 | Qtr 3, 2004 | Qtr 4, 2004 | |
| Jan | Feb | Mar | Apr | May | Jun | Jul | Aug | Sep | Oct | Nov | Dec |

**Figure 2-14: Three-Tiered Timescale Bar**

 The settings on the timescale bar apply to the active project only. To apply the three-tiered timescale bar to every future project, you must modify the timescale bar settings for each project template that you use.

# Module 03

# Inside Microsoft Project 2003

## *Learning Objectives*

After completing this module, you will be able to:

- Understand and explain the "YJTJ" Process
- Understand the Microsoft Project Data Model and how it affects Views, Tables, Filters, and Groups
- Select appropriate Views, Tables, Filters, and Groups
- Understand Single Views and Combination Views

# YJTJ Process (Your Job – Tool's Job)

Microsoft Project 2003 is a powerful tool for project management, but is very often misunderstood. Users tend to type in fields that, for the most part, they should leave for the tool to calculate. Although Microsoft Project 2003 is a powerful tool, it is not an intuitive tool. In fact, most software used for project management is not very intuitive.

In the defining and planning process, it is "Your Job" to gather project information and to enter this information in the proper places. Information you must gather includes the task list and resource list. It is the "Tool's Job" to use your information to create a schedule. Table 3-1 shows the YJTJ concept.

| **Y**our **J**ob | **T**ool's **J**ob |
|---|---|
| Provide Project Information | Create a Schedule |

**Table 3-1: The YJTJ Process**

# Microsoft Project Data Model

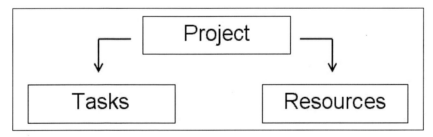

**Figure 3-1: Microsoft Project Data Model**

In the Microsoft Project data model shown in Figure 3-1, Microsoft Project 2003 recognizes two separate and distinct types of data: Task data and Resource data. Each type of data has its own unique set of Views, Tables, Filters, and Groups.

Task data carries Duration values measured by default in Days. Resource data carries Work (or Effort) values measured by default in Hours.

# Understanding Views

Microsoft Project 2003 offers 28 predefined Views, of which 22 are Task views and 6 are Resource views. The casual user of the software will define Views as "different ways of looking at my project information." Microsoft Project 2003 formally defines a View as:

**View = Table + Filter + Group + Screen**

You can display Views individually (a Single View) or in combination with another view (a Combination View). Views may contain a Gantt Chart, a timephased grid, or neither of these options. To select a View, do either of the following:

- Click the View menu, and then select one of the first 8 Views

- Click  View ➢ More Views, select the desired View, and then click the Apply button

 Microsoft Project 2003 contains four Views that you will use in PERT analysis. The first time you access one of these four PERT views, you must use the PERT Analysis toolbar to display them. After you display them the first time, the PERT views are available by clicking View ➢ More Views.

 Although it is possible to modify Views, MsProjectExperts recommends that you do not change any of the default Views included with the software. If a default View does not meet your communication or reporting needs, simply create a new View to meet such needs!

# Hands On Exercise

## Exercise 3-1

Apply task and resource Views in Microsoft Project 2003.

1. Open the student file called "Project Navigation.mpp"
2. Note that the software applies the Gantt Chart view by default
3. Apply and examine each of the following Views in this project:
   - Tracking Gantt
   - Task Usage
   - Resource Sheet
   - Resource Usage
4. Click View ➢ More Views
5. Select the Task Sheet view and then click Apply
6. Save, but do not close, the "Project Navigation.mpp" file

# Understanding Tables

Microsoft Project 2003 offers 31 predefined Tables, of which 21 are Task Tables and 10 are Resource Tables. By definition, a Table is simply a collection of fields (or columns). Fields display information such as Task Name, Duration, Start, Finish, Work, Cost, etc. Because the software displays Tables within Views, you must use task Tables with task Views, and resource Tables with resource Views. To apply a Table in the current View, do one of the following:

- Click View ➢ Table, and then select one of the Tables listed on the menu

- Click View ➢ Table ➢ More Tables, select one of the Tables listed, and click the Apply button

- Right-click on the Select All Button, and then either select a Table or select More Tables from the shortcut menu

 Microsoft Project 2003 contains four Tables that you will use in PERT analysis. The first time you access one of these four PERT Tables, you must use the PERT Analysis toolbar to display them. After you display them the first time, the PERT Tables are available by clicking View ➢ Table ➢ More Tables.

 Although it is possible to modify Tables, MsProjectExperts recommends that you do not change any of the default Tables included with the software. If a default Table does not meet your communication or reporting needs, simply create a new Table to meet such needs!

# Hands On Exercise

## Exercise 3-2

Apply task and resource Tables in Microsoft Project 2003.

1. Make sure that student file called "Project Navigation.mpp" is currently open

2. Right-click on the Select All button and note that the software applies the Entry table by default

3. Apply and examine each of the following task Tables:

   - Cost

   - Work

   - Variance

4. Click View ➢ Table ➢ More Tables

5. Select the Resource option at the top of the dialog box

6. Select the Usage table and then click Apply

Why does the software prevent you from applying the resource Usage table in this View?

Answer: _____

7. Select the Task option and apply the Entry table

8. Save, but do not close, the "Project Navigation.mpp" file

# Understanding Filters

Microsoft Project 2003 offers 56 predefined filters, of which 33 are task Filters and 23 are resource Filters. Filters allow you to extract specific information from Tables. Because Filters are associated with either Task data or Resource data, you must use task Filters with task Views and resource Filters with resource Views. To select a Filter, do one of the following:

- Click the Filter drop-down list on the Formatting toolbar and then select a Filter

- Click Project ➤ Filtered For and then select a Filter

- Click Project ➤ Filtered For ➤ More Filters, select a Filter, and then click either the Apply button or the Highlight button.

Any Filter name that ends with an ellipsis is as an "Interactive Filter." Interactive Filters prompt you for additional information before you can apply the Filter. The Created After... filter is an example of an Interactive Filter.

 When you click the Highlight button in the More Filters dialog box, Microsoft Project 2003 displays all tasks (or resources) but highlights in blue any data that meets your Filter criteria. When you do so, you have applied a Highlight Filter.

 Although it is possible to modify Filters, MsProjectExperts recommends that you do not change any of the default Filters included with the software. If a default Filter does not meet your communication or reporting needs, simply create a new Filter to meet such needs!

 Press the **F3** function key on your keyboard to apply the All Tasks filter.

# Hands On Exercise

## Exercise 3-3

Apply standard Filter in Microsoft Project 2003.

1. Make sure that student file called "Project Navigation.mpp" is currently open

2. Apply the Using Resource... filter

3. Select the resource named "Cher Zall" and click OK

4. Press the F3 function key to apply the All Tasks filter

## Exercise 3-4

Apply Highlight Filter in Microsoft Project 2003.

1. Click Project ➤ Filtered For ➤ More Filters

2. Select the Using Resource... filter and then click Highlight

3. Select Cher Zall and click OK

4. Note that this Highlight filter displays all tasks, but that Cher Zall's tasks are now highlighted in blue

5. Press the F3 function key to apply the All Tasks filter

6. Save, but do not close, the "Project Navigation.mpp" file

 To change the color used in a Highlight filter in any project, complete the following steps:

1. Click Format ➤ Text Styles

2. Select the Highlighted Tasks option in the Item to Change drop-down list

3. Select the desired Color option and then click OK

# Understanding Groups

Microsoft Project 2003 offers 15 predefined Groups, of which 9 are Task Groups and 6 are Resource Groups. You can use Groups to organize and sort task or resource information. To select a Group, do one of the following:

- Click the Group drop-down list on the Formatting toolbar and then select a Group

- Click Project ➤ Group by, and then select a Group

- Click Project menu ➤ Group by ➤ More Groups, select a Group and click the Apply button

Although it is possible to modify Groups, MsProjectExperts recommends that you do not change any of the default Groups included with the software. If a default Group does not meet your communication or reporting needs, simply create a new Group to meet such needs!

Press the **Shift+F3** keys on your keyboard to apply the group called No Group.

Many users do not find that the default Groups in Microsoft Project 2003 are very useful. However, you can use Groups most effectively when you create a custom Group and then apply the Group as a part of a custom View. Remember, the definition of a View is as follows:

View = Table + Filter + Group + Screen

# Hands On Exercise

## Exercise 3-5

Apply task and resource Groups in Microsoft Project 2003.

1. Make sure that student file called "Project Navigation.mpp" is currently open

2. Apply the Duration group

Note that the software has organized the task list into groups based on the Duration of each task

3. Apply the Resource Sheet view

4. Apply the group called Resource Group

5. Note that the software has organized the resources into groups based on their information in the Resource Group column

6. Reapply the Gantt Chart view

7. Save, but do not close, the "Project Navigation.mpp" file

# Single-Pane Views

In Microsoft Project 2003, a Single-Pane View is any View that displays in a single window. You can see the major single-pane views for both tasks and resources in Tables 3-2 and 3-3.

| Task Views | Consists Of |
|---|---|
| Gantt Chart | Task Sheet & Gantt Chart<br>Basic Task Information |
| Tracking Gantt | Task Sheet & Gantt Chart<br>Scheduled & Baseline Information |
| Task Sheet | Task Information<br>Displayed in Spreadsheet Format |
| Task Usage | Task Information<br>Assignment Information and Time-Phased Information |
| Task Form | Form displaying Task Details |

**Table 3-2: Major Task Views**

| Resource Views | Consists Of |
|---|---|
| Resource Sheet | Resource Information<br>Displayed in Spreadsheet Format |
| Resource Usage | Resource Information, Assignment Information, and Time-Phased Information |
| Resource Form | Form displaying Resource Details |

**Table 3-3: Major Resource Views**

# Combination Views

In Microsoft Project 2003, a Combination View is as any View that contains two Views, displayed in a split-screen format with each View in its own viewing pane. The View in the Bottom Pane displays detailed information about the selected Task, Resource, or Assignment in the View in the Top Pane. Table 3-4 describes the two major combination views in Microsoft Project 2003.

| Combination View | Consists Of |
|---|---|
| Task Entry | Gantt Chart and Task Form<br>Best Place for YJTJ Process! |
| Resource Allocation | Resource Usage and Leveling Gantt<br>Ideal for Leveling Resources |

**Table 3-4: Major Combination Views**

Figure 3-2 displays the Task Entry view, which is the most powerful combination View in Microsoft Project 2003. Notice in the lower pane that the software displays resource information about the task selected in the upper pane.

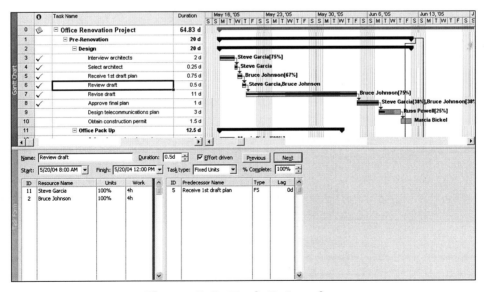

**Figure 3-2: Task Entry view**

**Hands On Exercise**

## Exercise 3-6

Apply two major combination Views in Microsoft Project 2003.

1. Make sure that student file called "Project Navigation.mpp" is currently open

2. Click Window ➤ Split to apply the Task Entry view

3. Select different tasks in the upper pane (one at a time) and note how this combination View functions

4. Apply the Resource Allocation view

5. Select different resources in the upper pane (one at a time) and note how this combination View functions

6. Close the lower pane

7. Apply the Gantt Chart view

8. Save and close "Project Navigation.mpp"

# Module 04

## Project Definition

### Learning Objectives

After completing this module, you will be able to:

- Understand the need for a project definition process
- Understand how to define a project in Microsoft Project 2003 using the msProjectExperts Six-Step Method

# The Need for a Project Definition Process

"The most important and difficult part of the project is its beginning...if done carefully, the project has a chance of success. If done carelessly, or not at all, the project is doomed to failure..."

*-- Effective Project Management* by Wysocki, Beck, and Crane

 As part of the project definition process, msProjectExperts recommends that a project manager should:

- Meet with all parties who have an interest in the project

- Document all project assumptions and constraints

- Clearly define the rules of engagement including change, issue, risk, acceptance, and completion criteria

# Project Definition in Microsoft Project 2003

Once your organization has properly defined the concept of the project, you are ready to define the project in Microsoft Project 2003. The six-step method recommend by msProjectExperts is an extremely effective way to define a project. These six steps are as follows:

1. Set the project Start date

2. Enter the project Properties

3. Display the Project Summary Task

4. Set the Project and Nonworking Time calendars

5. Set project Options unique to this project

6. Save the project

Completion of this six-step definition process will set the stage for the planning process, which includes task, resource, and assignment planning.

## Step #1 – Set the Project Start Date

When defining a new project in Microsoft Project 2003, the first step involves setting a project start date. When you set a project start date, the software will be able to calculate an estimated Finish date, based on the project information that you will enter during the task, resource, and assignment process.

 It may seem more logical to set a project Finish date and to let Microsoft Project 2003 calculate an estimated start date. More often than not, the result is an estimated start date that is already in the past. On many Y2K projects scheduled with a finish date, their project managers came to realize that their projects should have started months or even years earlier than they actually did!

To enter the project start date, complete the following steps:

1. Click the Project ➢ Project Information

2. Enter the Start date for your project and then click the OK button, as shown in Figure 4-1.

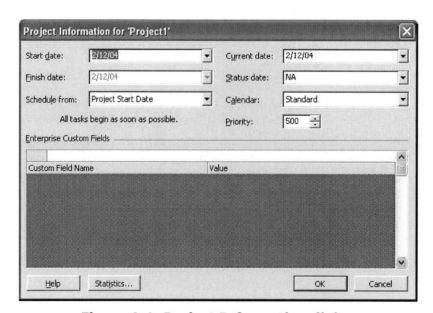

**Figure 4-1: Project Information dialog**

When you enter the project start date, click the Start date drop-down button to display the calendar date picker. You can then do either of the following:

- To quickly select a month, click the name of the month shown at the top of the calendar date picker

- To quickly select a year, click the year at the top of the calendar date picker

**Hands On Exercise**

## Exercise 4-1

You are as the project manager of the Project Master Rollout project to manage the deployment of the new enterprise project management software package. The contractual finish date for the project is June 29, 2007. Because of other commitments, the project team is not able to begin this project until January 2, 2007.

1. Open the file called "Project Master04" from your student folder

2. Click the Project ➢ Project Information

3. Set the project Start date to January 2, 2007

4. Click OK when finished

5. Save but *do not* close the "Project Master04" project file

## *Step #2 – Enter Properties*

Although you may overlook setting file Properties when creating a new Word document or Excel spreadsheet, it is important that you set the Properties for each new project you create in Microsoft Project 2003. The information you enter in the Properties, such as Title, Manager, and Company, the software automatically displays this information various places in the project, such as in Report headers and footers.

Figure 4-2 shows the Properties dialog for a new project. To set the Properties for a project, complete the following steps:

1. Click the File ➢ Properties
2. Enter project properties on the Summary page
3. Click OK when finished

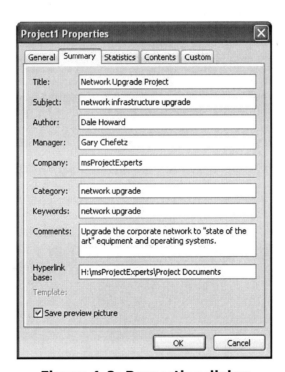

**Figure 4-2: Properties dialog**

Table 4-1 provides descriptions and recommendations for the use of project Property fields:

| Field Name | Description and Recommendations |
|---|---|
| Title | Displayed as the Task Name of the Project Summary Task (Row 0)<br><br>Displayed as the Task Name for subprojects inserted in a master project<br><br>Displayed in Views and Reports |
| Subject | Used for file searching when the project is saved as an .mpp file |
| Author | The person who maintains the project plan |
| Manager | Displayed in the headers and footers of Views and Reports<br><br>Used for file searching (.mpp files only) |
| Company | Displayed in the headers and footers of Views and Reports<br><br>Used for file searching (.mpp files only) |
| Category | Used for file searching (.mpp files only) |
| Keywords | Used for file searching (.mpp files only) |
| Comments | Displayed in the Notes field of the Project Summary Task (Row 0)<br><br>**Tip:** Copy and paste the first paragraph of the Executive Summary from the Statement of Work document |
| Hyperlink base | Displays the base path address for all relative hyperlinks inserted within the current document |
| Template | Displays the name of the Template from which you created the project plan (if you used a template) |
| Save preview picture | Saves a picture of the first page of your project file for previewing in the Open dialog box (.mpp files only) |

**Table 4-1: Project Properties fields**

# Hands On Exercise

## Exercise 4-2

Set the Properties for the Project Master project by completing the following steps.

1. Make sure you have the "Project Master04" project open

2. Click File ➢ Properties

3. In the Properties dialog box, set the Title as Project Master Rollout

4. Include other relevant information about this project from the paragraph in Exercise 4-1

5. Click the OK button when finished

6. Save but *do not* close the "Project Master04" project file

## Step #3 – Display the Project Summary Task

The Project Summary Task, also known as Row 0 or Task 0, is the highest-level summary task in your project. After you display the Project Summary Task and begin entering tasks, the software automatically indents all tasks at the first level of indenture. To display the Project Summary Task, complete the following steps:

1. Click Tools ➢ Options

2. Select the View page, if necessary

3. In the Outline Options section, select the Project summary task option

4. Click the OK button

Figure 4-3 shows the View page of the Options dialog, while Figure 4-4 shows the Project Summary Task (Row 0) in a project.

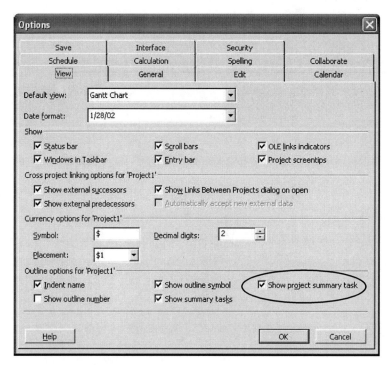

**Figure 4-3: Options dialog box, View page**

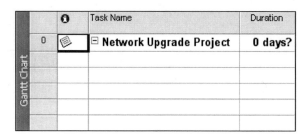

**Figure 4-4: Project Summary
Task (Row 0)**

# Hands On Exercise

## Exercise 4-3

Display the Project Summary Task (Row 0) in the Project Master project by completing the following steps.

1. Make sure you have the "Project Master04" project open

2. Click Tools ➢ Options

3. Select the View tab, if necessary

4. Select the Show project summary task option

5. Click OK

6. Save but *do not* close the "Project Master04" project file

## Step #4 –Set the Project Calendar and Nonworking Time Calendar

Microsoft Project 2003 uses the Project Calendar to govern the master working and nonworking schedule for every task in a project. You can select the Project Calendar from a list of base calendars available for that project. The Standard base calendar is the default Project Calendar for every new blank project in Microsoft Project 2003. To set a Project Calendar other than the Standard calendar, complete the following steps:

1. Click Project ➢ Project Information to display the Project Information dialog

2. Click the Calendar drop-down list at the bottom of the Project Information dialog box

3. Select the desired base calendar for scheduling the project, and then click OK

Notice in Figure 4-5 that I am selecting the MyCompany Standard calendar in the Project Information dialog box.

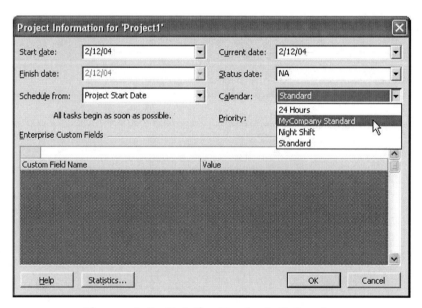

**Figure 4-5: Set the Project Calendar**

After selecting your desired base calendar as the Project Calendar, you must select the same base calendar as the Nonworking Time calendar. The Nonworking Time Calendar displays all nonworking dates as gray shaded bands on the Gantt Chart. To set the Nonworking Time calendar, complete the following steps:

1. Click Format ➢ Timescale to display the Timescale dialog

2. Select the Non-working time tab

3. Click the Calendar drop-down list, select the company calendar, and then click OK

Notice in Figure 4-6 that I have selected the MyCompany Standard calendar as the Nonworking Time Calendar in the Timescale dialog. Notice also that the software lists the MyCompany Standard calendar as the Project Calendar as well.

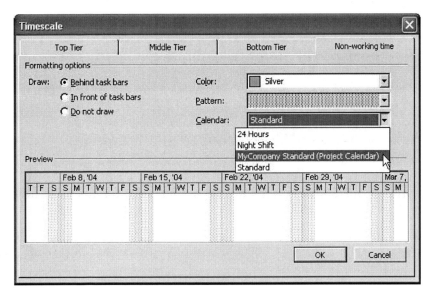

**Figure 4-6: Set the Nonworking Time Calendar**

 You can access the Timescale dialog box in two other ways:

- Double-click the timescale bar at the top of the Gantt Chart, then select the Nonworking Time tab, or

- Double-click any gray shaded band (nonworking time) in the Gantt Chart (fastest method)

# Hands On Exercise

## Exercise 4-4

Set the Project Calendar and the Non-Working Time Calendar for the Project Master project by completing the following steps.

1. Make sure you have the "Project Master04" project open

2. Click Project ➢ Project Information

3. Click the Calendar drop-down list and select the msPE Standard calendar

4. Click OK when finished

5. Double-click anywhere in one of the gray shaded non-working time bands on the Gantt Chart

6. Click the Calendar drop-down list and select the msPE Standard calendar

7. Click OK when finished

8. Save but *do not* close the "Project Master04" project file

# *Step #5 – Set Options Unique To This Project*

An important step in defining a new project is to set the project options that are unique to your project. Microsoft Project 2003 contains eleven pages of options in the Options dialog box, as shown in Figure 4-7. These options will allow you to define your project's appearance and to determine the behavior of the software.

Your knowledge of project options is critical for the effective use of Microsoft Project 2003. While most of the options are general in nature, others are very powerful from a scheduling, tracking, and informational standpoint. One important option, for example, is the standard Task Type for each task in your project. You will find this option on the Schedule page of the Options dialog.

To set project options, complete the following steps:

1. Click Tools ➢ Options

2. Select your desired options settings on each page, and then click OK

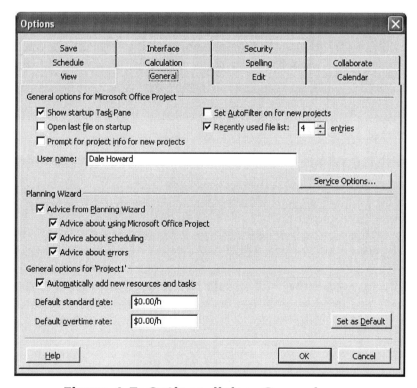

**Figure 4-7: Options dialog, General page**

The Options dialog box in Microsoft Project 2003 contains two types of options settings:

- Options that govern the display and behavior of the software regardless of which project is currently open

- Options that govern the behavior and display of the active project only

Pay close attention to the type of option that you are setting. If you set project-specific Options settings in one project and then open another project, your project-specific Options settings will not be present in the second project.

If you click the *Set as default* button in any of the project-specific sections of the Options dialog box, the settings you have selected will be set only in new projects. The software will not update your settings in pre-existing projects.

msProjectExperts recommends that you *do not* make changes to any of the Options settings unless you are absolutely certain about the impact of the changes. Because many of the Options settings are global in nature, making one change in a project Option could affect all of your projects.

As part of your company's Microsoft Project 2003 methodologies, msProjectExperts recommends that Options settings be determined for your organization and then distributed to all users of the software.

The following pages document the msProjectExperts recommended settings that differ from the default settings on each page in the Options dialog box.

| View Options | |
|---|---|
| **Option** | **Option Setting** |
| Date format: | 1/28/02 |
| Show project summary task | Checked |

| General Options | |
|---|---|
| **Option** | **Option Setting** |
| Show startup Task Pane | Unchecked |
| Recently used file list: | 9 entries |
| User name: | Type your name here |
| Automatically add new resources and tasks | Unchecked and Set as Default |

| Edit Options | |
|---|---|
| **Option** | **Option Setting** |
| Minutes: | m |
| Hours: | h |
| Days: | d |
| Weeks: | w |
| Months: | mo |
| Years: | Y |
| View options section | Set as Default |

When setting the values for the Time Units options, click the OK button before selecting any other page in the Options dialog box. Otherwise, the software resets your Time Units settings back to their defaults.

| Schedule Options | |
| --- | --- |
| **Option** | **Option Setting** |
| Show that tasks have estimated durations | Unchecked |
| New tasks have estimated durations | Unchecked |
| Scheduling options section | Set as Default |

| Interface Options | |
| --- | --- |
| **Option** | **Option Setting** |
| Display Project Guide | Unchecked |

 The Options dialog contains a new Security page. Set your Security options according to your company's IT security policies.

# Hands On Exercise

## Exercise 4-5

Set the project options for this project by completing the following steps.

1. Make sure you have the "Project Master04" project open

2. Click Tools ➢ Options

3. Set the msProjectExperts recommended Options detailed on the previous two pages

4. Click OK when finished

5. Save but *do not* close the "Project Master04" project file

## *Step #6 – Save the Project*

The final step in the definition process is to save the project plan according to your company's methodologies for naming convention. To do this, complete the following steps:

1. Click File ➤ Save

2. In the Save As dialog, type a name for your project that conforms to your company's naming convention

3. Click the Save button

Figure 4-8 shows the Save As dialog.

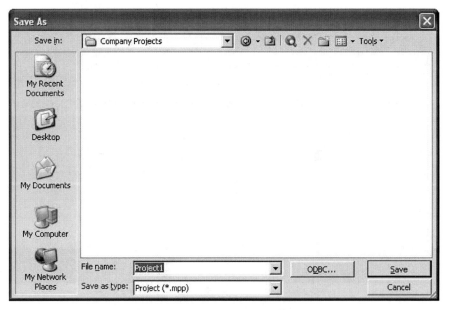

**Figure 4-8: Save As dialog**

 If you save your file as an .mpp file, Microsoft Project 2003 uses the same file format as Microsoft Project 2000. This means that you can do the following:

1. Save a project using Microsoft Project 2003

2. Open it, revise it, and save using Microsoft Project 2000 or 2002

3. Reopen it using Microsoft Project 2003

When a user opens a Project 2003 file in Project 2000, the software will hide all data fields specific to Project 2003.

**Hands On Exercise**

## Exercise 4-6

The naming convention for msPE project files includes the department, the 3-letter initials of the project manager, and a brief description of the project in the file name. Save this project file using the company naming convention.

1. Make sure you have the "Project Master04" project open

2. Click File ➢ Save As

3. In the Save As dialog box, save your file using the company's naming convention (use your real department name, your own three-letter initials, and a short description of the project)

4. Click the Save button when finished

5. Close the renamed "Project Master04" project file

# More About Base Calendars

A base calendar is a master calendar which represents the working and nonworking schedule for employees in your company. Microsoft Project 2003 uses base calendars to schedule all work on a project and to set the working and nonworking schedule of each resource as well.

In an enterprise environment with Microsoft Project 2003, your Project Server administrator will create enterprise base calendars for you and you may not be able to create your own base calendars. In a non-enterprise environment, however, you can still create your own base calendars. The following material in this module documents how to create your own base calendars.

Microsoft Project 2003 offers three predefined base calendars: a 24 Hours calendar, a Night Shift calendar, and a Standard calendar. The Standard calendar is set as the default Project Calendar. The working schedule on the Standard calendar is Monday through Friday from 8:00 AM – 12:00 PM, and 1:00 PM – 5:00 PM, with Saturdays and Sundays set as Nonworking time.

## *Creating a Base Calendar*

Rather than using any of the predefined calendars, msProjectExperts recommends that you create a new base calendar, preferably named after your company, business unit, or department. All national and company holidays should be entered in the new base calendar, as well as customized working hours for selected days. Creating a new base calendar guarantees that your projects will reflect your company's schedule for both working time and nonworking time.

To create a new base calendar, complete the following steps:

1. Click Tools ➢ Change Working Time

The Change Working Time dialog displays, as is shown in Figure 4-9.

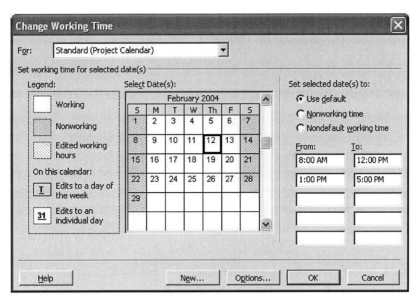

**Figure 4-9: Change Working Time dialog**

2.  In the Change Working Time dialog box, click the New button

The Create New Base Calendar dialog displays, as is shown in Figure 4-10.

**Figure 4-10: Create New Base
Calendar dialog**

3.  Type a Name for your new base calendar
4.  Select the Create new base calendar option
5.  Click OK

 You also have the option of making a copy of an existing calendar, which duplicates the schedule from an existing calendar to the new calendar. This option is very helpful when you have already created your company's base calendar, but also need to create additional calendars for employees who work a different schedule, such a workweek with four 10-hour days.

To set dates as national holidays, company holidays, or other nonworking time, continue with the following steps:

6. Select the desired date

7. Click Nonworking time option in the Set selected date(s) to: section

For example, in Figure 4-11 I am setting July 4, 2005 as a company holiday.

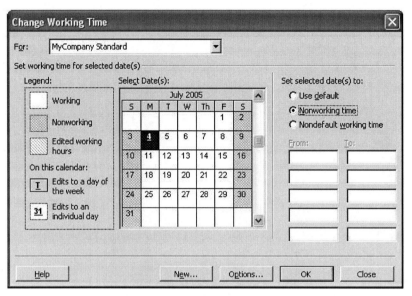

**Figure 4-11: Set July 4, 2005
as nonworking time**

 To set consecutive nonworking days, drag to select each day and then click Nonworking time. To select noncontiguous dates, select the first date, press and hold the Ctrl key while selecting additional dates, and then click Nonworking time.

8. When you have finished setting your working and nonworking schedule, click the OK button

# Hands On Exercise

## Exercise 4-7

Create a new base calendar.

1. Open the file called "Create a Calendar" from your student folder

2. Create a new base calendar and name it using the initials for your company

3. Set the following company holidays as nonworking time for the upcoming calendar year on your new base calendar:

   - President's Day – Third Monday of February
   - Memorial Day – the last Monday in May
   - Independence Day
   - Company picnic (afternoon off) – First Friday in August
   - Labor Day – the first Monday in September
   - Thanksgiving – the fourth Thursday in November
   - The Friday following Thanksgiving
   - Christmas Eve (afternoon off)
   - Christmas Day
   - New Years Eve (afternoon off)
   - New Years Day

4. Save and close your "Create a Calendar" file

# Module 05

## Project Planning – Tasks

### Learning Objectives

After completing this module, you will be able to:

- Understand the task planning process
- Create project tasks and build the Work Breakdown Structure
- Create project milestones
- Set task dependencies, constraints, and deadline dates
- Document the task list with appropriate task notes

# The Task Planning Process

Once a project has been defined, the planning process begins. The first step in the planning process is task planning. You can create a list of tasks in a project in Microsoft Project 2003 by either typing the list manually or by using a template.

## *Creating a Task List Manually*

To manually create a task list requires thoughtful analysis of the activity needs of the project and lots of typing! You can use either a "top down" or "bottom up" approach to create the initial task list. The "top down" approach begins by listing the major phases of the project, as well as the project deliverables under each phase. You will then list the activities under each deliverable which are necessary to produce the deliverable. The "bottom up" approach works in the opposite direction. Using this approach, you will list all of the activities in the project and then organize the activities into deliverables and phases. Either approach is effective in creating the task list for the project.

Whenever you need to create a new project manually, it is a good idea to follow this methodology:

1. Create the task list
2. Create phases and deliverables to generate the project's Work Breakdown Structure (WBS)
3. Create project milestones
4. Set task dependencies, including lag time if necessary
5. Document unusual task dependencies with a task Note
6. Set task constraints and deadline dates wherever needed
7. Document all task constraints with a task Note
8. Set task Calendars for any task with an alternate working schedule
9. Document task Calendars with a task Note

## *Using a Template*

The easiest way to create the project's task list is to use a template. Generally speaking, most templates contain a generic list of tasks for a certain type of project, along with the WBS, milestones, and task dependencies. You probably will not be able to use a template "out of the box" and will need to delete tasks, add new tasks, and set task constraints, wherever appropriate.

Templates are generally created in one of two ways:

- Convert the project plan from a successful project to a template
- Create a template from scratch, based on the needs of a company, department, or project team

 If templates do not currently exist in your organization, msProjectExperts recommends that you identify common project types and then create appropriate project templates.

 The Tasks section of the Project Guide sidepane offers a series of steps for task planning, including:

- List the tasks in the project
- Organize tasks into phases
- Schedule tasks
- Link or attach more task information
- Set deadlines and constrain tasks

 Microsoft Project 2003 offers two other methods for creating the task list in a project plan: importing tasks from either a Microsoft Excel workbook or from Microsoft Outlook. To import tasks from Excel, click the List the tasks in the project hyperlink in the Project Guide sidepane, then click the Import wizard hyperlink in the "Import Tasks from Excel" section. To import tasks from Outlook, click the Tools ➤ Import Outlook Tasks.

# Planning for Non-Deliverable Tasks

In the planning process, all activities related to the project should be listed in the project plan; however, non-deliverable tasks are often overlooked. Non-deliverable tasks are usually one of two types: support tasks or recurring tasks. Support tasks include project support activities such as project management tasks and project administration. Recurring tasks, such as status meetings, may also be included in the project plan. The frequency of recurring tasks must be adequate for reviewing and reporting project progress.

# Basic Task Skills

To be able to use Microsoft Project 2003 effectively, you should possess a variety of basic task skills, such as entering and editing tasks, moving tasks, creating Milestone tasks, creating the Work Breakdown Structure (WBS), etc. We will discuss each of the basic task planning skills in the following sections.

## *Entering and Editing Tasks*

Entering tasks in Microsoft Project 2003 is very similar to entering data in a Microsoft Excel spreadsheet. To enter a new task, complete the following steps:

1. Select a blank cell in the Task Name column of the Task Sheet
2. Type the task name
3. Press the Enter key or Down-Arrow key on the keyboard

To edit a task once it has been entered, select the task to be edited and then use any of the following methods:

- Retype the task name
- Press the F2 key on the keyboard and edit the task name
- Click anywhere in the Entry Bar and edit the task name

The Entry Bar during the editing process is shown in Figure 5-1.

**Figure 5-1: Entry Bar
while editing a task**

# Hands On Exercise

## Exercise 5-1

Use basic task planning skills to define the task list in the Project Master Rollout project.

1.  Open the file called "Project Master05" from your student folder

2.  In the blank cells at the bottom of the existing task list, add the following new tasks:

    Load and Configure Software
    Determine Server Specifications
    Provide Training
    Testing Complete

3.  Edit the task, Conduct Skills Accessment, and change "Accessment" to "Assessment"

4.  "Best Fit" the Task Name column and dock the split bar on the right edge of the Duration column, if necessary

5.  Save but *do not* close your "Project Master 05" project file

## *Moving Tasks*

During the task planning process, you will probably create the task list with some tasks out of order. Rearranging tasks in Microsoft Project 2003 is definitely not an "intuitive" skill. To move a task, complete the following steps:

1. Click once on the Task ID Number indicator (row header) on the far left end of the task to select the entire task

2. Click and hold the Task ID Number indicator to "grab" the task

3. Move the mouse pointer up or down on the screen to move the task

As you move the mouse pointer, you will see a gray I-beam bar to indicate that the task is being moved, as shown in Figure 5-2.

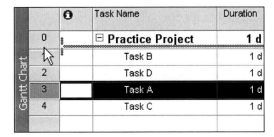

**Figure 5-2: Moving a Task**

4. Drag the task until the gray I-beam indicator is positioned where you want the task to be placed

5. Release the mouse button to complete the move and drop the task in its new location

# Hands On Exercise

## Exercise 5-2

Rearrange the task list into a meaningful order by completing the following steps.

1. Make sure that the "Project Master05" file is open

2. Rearrange the tasks in the Project Master project into the following order:

   INSTALLATION

   Determine Server Specifications
   Order Server
   Setup Server and Load O/S
   Load and Configure Software
   Installation Complete

   TESTING

   Setup Test Clients
   Verify Connectivity
   Testing Complete

   TRAINING

   Create Training Materials
   Conduct Skills Assessment
   Create Training Schedule
   Provide Training
   Project Complete

3. Save but *do not* close your "Project Master 05" project file

## *Inserting Tasks*

Occasionally while entering a task list, you will discover that you have left out one or more tasks that you should have entered elsewhere in the task list. To insert new tasks in your project plan, complete the following steps:

1. Select any cell in the row where the new task should be inserted

2. Press the Insert key on the keyboard or click Insert ➤ New Task

Microsoft Project 2003 will automatically add a new blank task row at the selected point, and all of the following tasks will be shifted down one row. To add multiple new tasks simultaneously, select as many rows as the number of new tasks you would like to add, and then press the Insert key.

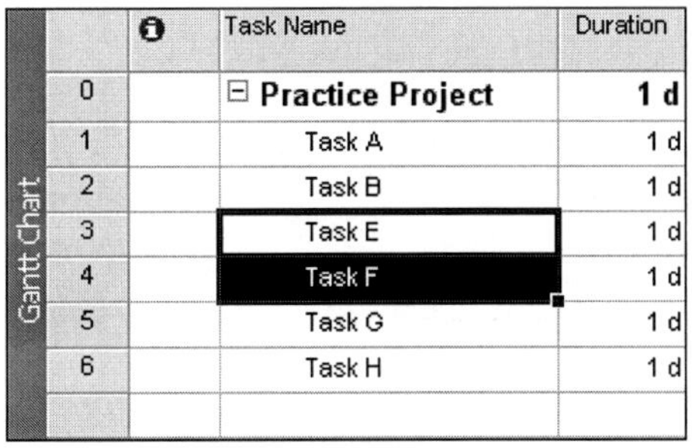

| | | ⓘ | Task Name | Duration |
|---|---|---|---|---|
| | 0 | | ⊟ **Practice Project** | **1 d** |
| | 1 | | Task A | 1 d |
| | 2 | | Task B | 1 d |
| | 3 | | Task E | 1 d |
| | 4 | | Task F | 1 d |
| | 5 | | Task G | 1 d |
| | 6 | | Task H | 1 d |
| | | | | |

**Figure 5-3: Preparing to insert two
new tasks before Task E**

In Figure 5-3, I want to add two new tasks after Task B, so I have selected Tasks E and F as the location of the new tasks. Once I have done so, I can quickly insert the two new tasks by pressing the Insert key on the keyboard. Microsoft Project 2003 will automatically insert two new blank rows and shift all of the following rows down, as shown in Figure 5-4.

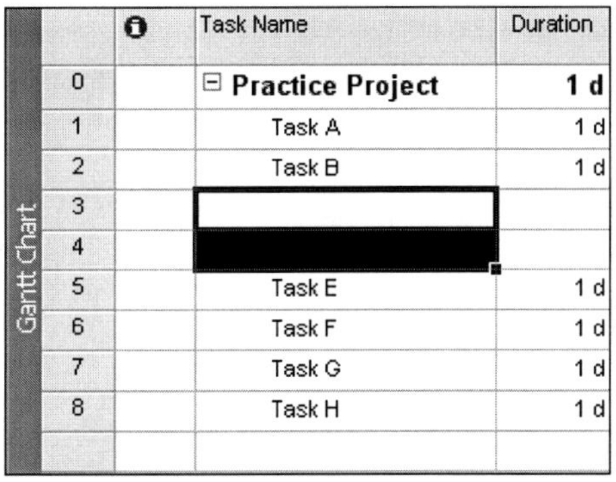

| | | ⓘ | Task Name | Duration |
|---|---|---|---|---|
| | 0 | | ⊟ **Practice Project** | **1 d** |
| | 1 | | Task A | 1 d |
| | 2 | | Task B | 1 d |
| | 3 | | | |
| | 4 | | | |
| | 5 | | Task E | 1 d |
| | 6 | | Task F | 1 d |
| | 7 | | Task G | 1 d |
| | 8 | | Task H | 1 d |
| | | | | |

**Figure 5-4: Two new tasks
inserted before Task E**

# Hands On Exercise

## Exercise 5-3

Members of the Test team have determined that a task is missing in the Testing section of the project. The task, Troubleshoot Errors, needs to be added between the tasks Verify Connectivity and Testing Complete. Add this new task to the project by completing the following steps.

1. Make sure that the "Project Master05" file is open

2. Select the task, Testing Complete

3. Press the Insert key on the keyboard

4. In the new blank cell, add a task named Troubleshoot Errors and press the Enter key

5. Save but *do not* close your "Project Master 05" project file

## *Deleting Tasks*

Occasionally while entering a task list, you will find one or more tasks that are no longer needed in the project plan. To delete a task in your project plan, complete the following steps:

1. Click ID number for the task you want to delete (this will select the entire task)

2. Press the Delete key on the keyboard or click Edit ➢ Delete Task

If you select any cell in the Task Name column and press the Delete key, the software displays a Smart Tag to the left of the cell. The Smart Tag allows you to select whether to clear the contents of only that cell or to delete the entire task.

 The use of Smart Tags is one common feature between Microsoft Project 2003 and Microsoft Office XP/2003.

In Figure 5-5, I have selected the Smart Tag to delete the entire task.

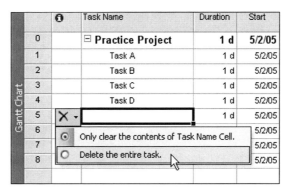

**Figure 5-5: Smart Tag after a
deletion in the Task Name column**

 In any Resource view, if you select a cell in the Resource Name column and press the Delete key, you will also see Smart Tag to the left of the cell. The choices are similar to those offered while deleting a cell in any Task view.

**Hands On Exercise**

## Exercise 5-4

Members of the project team have concluded that the server specifications are already known for this project; therefore, the Determine Server Specifications task will not be needed. Delete this task from the project by completing the following steps.

1. Make sure that the "Project Master05" file is open

2. Select the ID number for the task, Determine Server Specifications, to highlight the entire task

3. Press the Delete key on the keyboard

4. Save but *do not* close your "Project Master 05" project file

## *Creating the Work Breakdown Structure (WBS)*

The Work Breakdown Structure (WBS) divides the project activities into meaningful components. The WBS consists of summary tasks (phases and deliverables) and subtasks (activities). A generic Work Breakdown Structure (WBS) is shown in Figure 5-6.

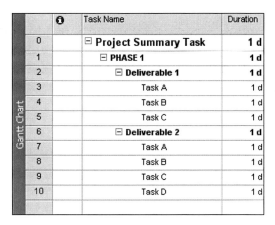

**Figure 5-6: Work Breakdown
Structure**

To create the Work Breakdown Structure (WBS) with Phases and Deliverables, you will need to create a series of summary tasks and subtasks. The purpose of summary tasks is to summarize or "roll up" the data contained in the Subtasks.

In Figure 5-7, I want to make the PHASE I task a summary task and make Tasks A through D subtasks of the PHASE I summary task. To do so, I must select Task A through Task D and then click the Indent button on the Formatting toolbar.

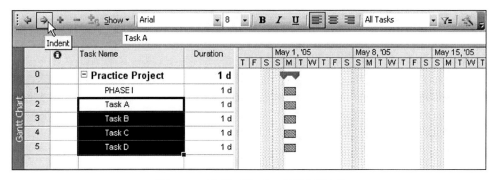

**Figure 5-7: Make PHASE I
a Summary Task**

To create a Summary Task, complete the following steps:

1. Select or highlight those tasks which will become subtasks of the summary task

2. Click the Indent button on the Formatting toolbar

Once these steps are completed, the selected tasks will become subtasks of the task immediately preceding them, which then becomes a summary task. Microsoft Project 2003 gives the user multiple clues to distinguish between regular tasks and Summary Tasks. Notice some of those clues in Figure 5-8.

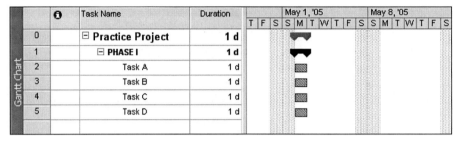

**Figure 5-8: PHASE I is a summary task
while Tasks A-D are subtasks**

Notice in Figure 5-8 how Microsoft Project 2003 displays Summary Tasks and Subtasks:

- PHASE I is formatted in bold

- There is an outline indicator in front of the task name PHASE I

- The Gantt bar for PHASE I is an unusual jagged shape

- Tasks A-D are indented one level further than PHASE I

 Microsoft Project 2003 supports 65,535 levels of indenture! Indenting is also known as "Demoting" tasks. Outdenting is also known as "Promoting" tasks.

# Hands On Exercise

## Exercise 5-5

Organize the Project Master project into phases and subtasks by creating the Work Breakdown Structure (WBS) for the project.

1. Make sure that the "Project Master05" file is open

2. Indent tasks #2-4 to make the INSTALLATION task a summary task

3. Indent tasks #7-9 to make the TESTING task a summary task

4. Indent tasks #12-15 to make the TRAINING task a summary task

5. "Best Fit" the Task Name column and drag the vertical split bar to the right of the Duration column, if necessary

6. Confirm that tasks #5, 10, and 16 are not indented and at the same level of indenture as the three summary tasks

Your task list should appear as displayed in Figure 5-9.

| | ⓘ | Task Name | Duration | Dec 31, '06 |
|---|---|---|---|---|
| 0 | 📋 | ⊟ **Project Master Rollout** | **1 d** | |
| 1 | | ⊟ **INSTALLATION** | **1 d** | |
| 2 | | Order Server | 1 d | |
| 3 | | Setup Server and Load O/S | 1 d | |
| 4 | | Load and Configure Software | 1 d | |
| 5 | | Installation Complete | 1 d | |
| 6 | | ⊟ **TESTING** | **1 d** | |
| 7 | | Setup Test Clients | 1 d | |
| 8 | | Verify Connectivity | 1 d | |
| 9 | | Troubleshoot Errors | 1 d | |
| 10 | | Testing Complete | 1 d | |
| 11 | | ⊟ **TRAINING** | **1 d** | |
| 12 | | Create Training Materials | 1 d | |
| 13 | | Conduct Skills Assessment | 1 d | |
| 14 | | Create Training Schedule | 1 d | |
| 15 | | Provide Training | 1 d | |
| 16 | | Project Complete | 1 d | |

**Figure 5:9 Task list with Work Breakdown Structure applied**

## Creating Milestones

In project management term, a Milestone is defined as "a significant point in time" in a project plan. You can use a Milestone to indicate the beginning point of a project, the ending point for a phase or a deliverable, and even the ending point for an entire project. Most projects contain multiple Milestones.

In Microsoft Project 2003, to convert any task to a Milestone, simply change its Duration to 0 Days. Notice in Figure 5-10 that the Gantt Chart symbol for a Milestone is a black diamond which carries the finish date of the Milestone.

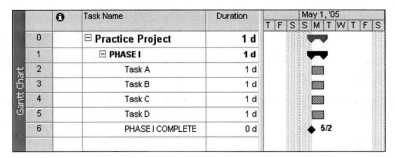

**Figure 5-10: PHASE I COMPLETE
is a Milestone**

# Hands On Exercise

## Exercise 5-6

Create Milestones to denote the completion date of each summary
task in the Project Master Rollout project.

1. Make sure that the "Project Master05" file is open

2. Change the Duration of the Installation Complete task to 0 days
   and then press the Enter key

3. Select the Testing Complete task, press the Control key, and
   then simultaneously select the Project Complete task

4. Click the Task Information button on the Standard toolbar

5. In the Multiple Task Information dialog box, set the Duration of
   both tasks to 0 days, and then click the OK button

6. Save but *do not* close your "Project Master05" project plan

## *Creating Recurring Tasks*

In Microsoft Project 2003, a Recurring Task is any task that repeats regularly. You can use Recurring Tasks for meetings and other events that occur at regular intervals. You can insert Recurring Tasks anywhere in a project plan, although many people prefer to insert them at the beginning or end of the task list. To insert a Recurring Task into a project plan, complete the following steps:

1. Select the location in the project where you would like to have the Recurring Task inserted
2. Click Insert ➢ Recurring Task
3. In the Recurring Task Information Dialog Box, enter the Name of the Recurring Task
4. Enter the Duration of the Recurring Task (normally in hours)
5. Enter a Recurrence Pattern (how often the task occurs and when it occurs during the pattern selected)
6. Enter the Range of Recurrence (when the first task occurs and how many occurrences)
7. Click the OK button

In Figure 5-11, I have created a Recurring Task called "Monthly Budget Review." This 3-hour meeting will occur the last Friday of every month, and is scheduled for 6 occurrences from 5/2/05 (the first month of the project) through 10/28/05 (the last anticipated month of the project).

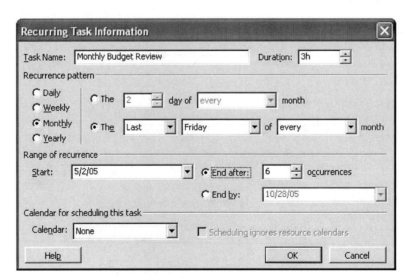

**Figure 5-11: Recurring Task
Information dialog**

When this Recurring Task is inserted into a project plan, it appears as shown in Figure 5-12.

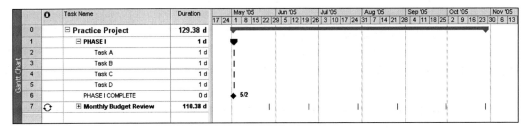

**Figure 5-12: Monthly Budget
Review recurring task**

In Figure 5-12, notice the special indicator for a Recurring Task in the Indicators column, and that the monthly meeting occurrences are scheduled for the next six months.

# Hands On Exercise

## Exercise 5-7

The team leaders from the project team must attend a 2-hour project status meeting every Monday during the life of the project. Therefore, create a recurring task in the Project Master Rollout project to account for these project status meetings.

1. Make sure that the "Project Master05" file is open

2. Select the INSTALLATION summary task

3. Click Insert ➢ Recurring Task

4. Create the recurring task using the following information:

   - **Name** – Project Status Meeting
   - **Duration** – 2h
   - **Recurrence Pattern** – Weekly
   - Every week on Monday
   - **Start** – 1/8/07
   - **End after** – 25 occurrences

5. When prompted about rescheduling Project Status Meetings that fall on a nonworking time period, click the Yes button

6. Save but *do not* close your "Project Master05" project plan

## *Adding Task Notes*

Task Notes are an important part of project documentation and are essential to understanding the historical information about any project. You can add Notes to tasks at any time during the life of the project, including during defining, planning, execution, and even at closure. To add a Note to a task, select a task and then use any of the following methods:

- Click Project ➢ Task Notes

- Double-click the task and then click the Notes tab

- Click the Notes button on the Standard toolbar

The software displays the Notes page as one of five tabs in the Task Information dialog box as shown in Figure 5-13. Type the text of the note, add formatting as desired, and then click the OK button.

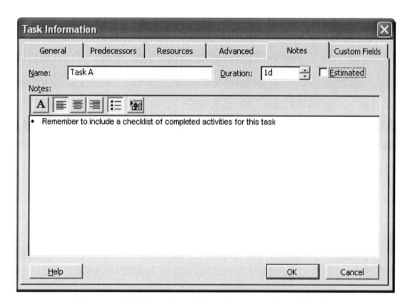

**Figure 5-13: Task Information dialog
Notes Page**

When you have added Notes to a task, a Note indicator will appear in the Indicators column to the left of the task, as is shown in Figure 5-14. You can read the text of the Note by floating your mouse pointer over the Note indicator.

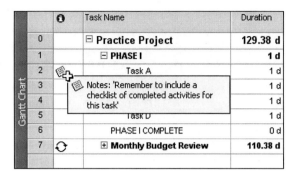

**Figure 5-14: Notes Indicator with
Screen Tip text displayed**

 msProjectExperts recommends that you use "bulleted" text for your text Notes, as shown previously in the Figure 5-13. When a task contains multiple Notes, the bulleted text will make the individual Notes easier to read, and will print much better in standard and custom Reports.

**Hands On Exercise**

## Exercise 5-8

Add a task Note to the Setup Test Clients task, indicating the location of the installation script on the company network.

1. Double-click the task Setup Test Clients

2. Click the Notes tab

3. Click the Bulleted List button

4. In the Notes text box, type the following text: "Installation script is stored at H:\proj_mgmt\pm."

5. Click OK

6. Place your cursor over the Notes indicator to view the Note on the Setup Test Clients task

# Setting Task Dependencies

Following the completion of the WBS, your next step in the task planning process is to determine the order in which tasks will occur. This process is formally known as Activity Sequencing, which involves identifying and documenting interactivity dependencies.

Task dependencies can be mandatory, discretionary, and external. An example of a mandatory dependency would be "Pour Floors" prior to "Put up Walls"; while an example of a discretionary dependency would be "Install Electrical" prior to "Install Plumbing." An example of an external dependency would be "Acquire Server" in one project plan prior to "Load Software" in a separate (external) project plan.

In the real world, there are some tasks that have no dependency on any other tasks. In fact, some tasks will happen independently of other tasks which are in the same phase or deliverable. In situations like these, do not set a dependency on a task which has no dependency relationship with other tasks. Only set dependencies where a true "hard logic" dependency relationship exists between tasks!

 msProjectExperts recommends the use of mandatory dependencies wherever possible for tasks that are truly dependant on each other in nature. Using discretionary dependencies may cause scheduling problems later in the project.

Microsoft Project 2003 offers the following task dependency types:

- A **Finish-to-Start (FS)** dependency means that the Predecessor task must finish before the Successor task can start. Figure 5-15 shows an FS dependency between Task A and Task B.

| | ❶ | Task Name | Duration | Jun 4, '06 | Jun 11, '06 | Jun 18, '06 |
|---|---|---|---|---|---|---|
| 1 | | Task A | 7 d | | | |
| 2 | | Task B | 7 d | | | |

**Figure 5-15: Finish to Start Dependency
between Tasks A and B**

- A **Start-to-Start (SS)** dependency means that the Predecessor task must start before the Successor task can start. Figure 5-16 shows an SS dependency between Task A and Task B.

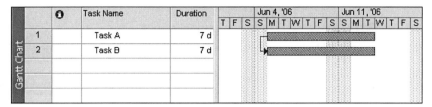

**Figure 5-16: Start to Start Dependency
between Tasks A and B**

 A Start-to-Start relationship does not mean that the predecessor and successor *must* start at the same time. It simply means that successor task may start any time *after* the predecessor starts.

- A **Finish-to-Finish (FF)** dependency means that the Predecessor task must finish before the Successor task can finish. Figure 5-17 shows an FF dependency between Task A and Task B.

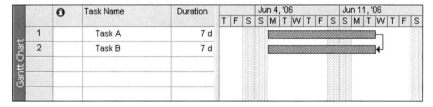

**Figure 5-17: Finish to Finish Dependency
between Tasks A and B**

 A Finish-to-Finish relationship does not mean that the predecessor and successor *must* finish at the same time. It simply means that the successor task may finish any time *after* the predecessor finishes.

- A **Start-to-Finish (SF)** means that the Predecessor task must start before the Successor task can finish. This dependency is rarely used, but it can be needed in certain situations. Figure 5-18 shows an SF dependency between Task A and Task B.

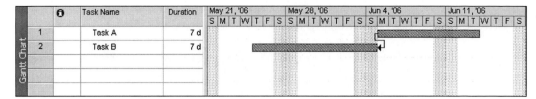

**Figure 5-18: Start to Finish Dependency
between Tasks A and B**

To set a dependency in Microsoft Project 2003, complete the following steps:

1. Select one or more tasks which are dependent
2. Click the Link Tasks button on the Standard toolbar

When you have completed these steps, the software sets the default dependency type, which is the Finish-to-Start (FS) dependency. To change the dependency type to any of the other three, do the following:

1. Double-click the link line between the dependent tasks
2. In the Task Dependency dialog box, select the desired dependency type and click the OK button

To remove a dependency relationship between two or more tasks, complete the following steps:

1. Select the tasks from which to remove the dependencies
2. Click the Unlink Tasks button on the Standard toolbar

## *Lag Time*

Lag Time is defined as a delay in the start of a Successor task. You can use Lag Time for a number of reasons, including:

- To manage project risk based on the degree of risk on the finish date of the Predecessor task
- To account for a delay in the delivery of equipment or supplies
- To allow a portion (time or percentage) of the Predecessor task to be completed before the Successor task begins

You can enter Lag Time as either a time value, such as 5 days, or as a percentage of the Duration of the predecessor task. In Figure 5-19, I have added 3 days of Lag Time to the FS dependency so that Task B will start 3 days after Task F is finished.

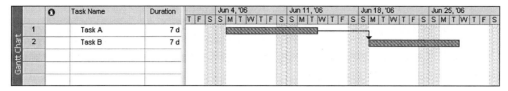

**Figure 5-19: 3-Day Lag applied to
an FS dependency**

In the Figure 5-20, I have added 75% Lag Time to the SS dependency, so
that Task B will not begin until Task A has started and 75% of Task A has
been completed.

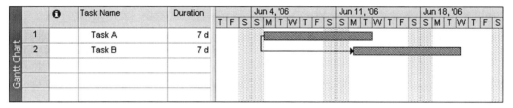

**Figure 5-20: 75% Lag applied
to an SS dependency**

To enter Lag Time, double-click the link line between two dependent tasks,
and then enter a Lag value (either as a time unit, such as days, or as a
percentage) in the Task Dependency dialog, as shown in Figure 5-21.

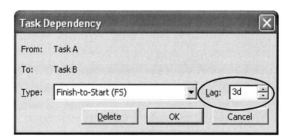

**Figure 5-21: Task Dependency
dialog box**

You can also add Lag time in the Predecessors column of the
task Entry table, using notation such as "1FS+3d", which
would mean that task ID #1 is a predecessor to the selected
task, in a Finish to Start dependency with a Lag time of 3
days.

## *Lead Time*

Lead Time is the opposite of Lag Time and creates an overlap between linked tasks. In an FS dependency, a three-day lead means the successor task is scheduled to start three days prior to the finish of the predecessor task. Lead Time is expressed as a negative lag value, either measured as a time unit (such as days) or as a percentage.

In Figure 5-22, I have set 3 days of Lead Time to the FS dependency, which creates an overlap between Tasks A and B.

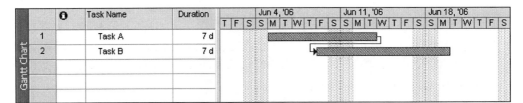

**Figure 5-22: FS Dependency with 3 day Lead**

 Lead Time is used to "fast track" a project by compressing the time it will take to complete a project schedule. FS dependencies with lead time are Discretionary dependencies, which may cause scheduling problems. msProjectExperts advises you to be very careful when using Lead Time in your projects!

# Hands On Exercise

## Exercise 5-9

Set task dependencies in your Project Master Rollout project.

1. Link task ID's #28-31 with a Finish to Start (FS) dependency

Because of the delay between when the server is ordered and when it is actually delivered, Lag time will need to be added to the FS dependency between the task Order Server and the task Setup Server and Load O/S.

2. Set an 8-day Lag on the FS dependency between task ID's #28 and #29

3. Link task ID's #33-36 with a Finish to Start (FS) dependency

4. Link task ID's #38-42 with a Finish to Start (FS) dependency

The task, Conduct Skills Assessment, can begin once 90% of the task, Create Training Materials, has been completed.

5. Set a *-10% Lag* on the FS dependency between task ID's #38 and #39

The task, Provide Training, cannot begin until 5 days after the task, Create Training Schedule, has been completed.

6. Set a 5-day Lag on the FS dependency between task ID's #40 and #41

7. Link task ID's #31 and #33 with a Finish to Start (FS) dependency

8. Link task ID's #36 and #38 with a Finish to Start (FS) dependency

9. Save but *do not* close your "Project Master05" project plan

Your Project Master Rollout project should appear as is shown in Figure 5-23.

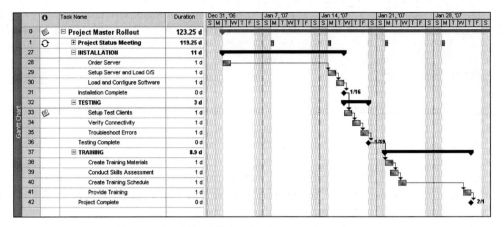

**Figure 5-23: All task dependencies set**

# Setting Task Constraints

A constraint is a restriction or limitation that you set on the start date or finish date of a task. When you set a constraint on a task in Microsoft Project 2003, you are restricting the ability of the task's start date or finish date from moving automatically in time. You will probably use Constraints for issues like:

- Deadline dates for the completion of tasks

- Delivery dates for equipment and supplies

- Resource availability restrictions

For example, the project sponsor might set a deadline date on the completion of a certain task in your project, requiring you to set a Finish No Later Than constraint on that task.

To set a Constraint on a task, complete the following steps:

1. Double-click the task to be constrained

2. In the Task Information dialog box, click the Advanced tab

3. Click the Constraint Type drop-down list and select a constraint

4. Click the Constraint Date drop-down calendar and select a date for the constraint

5. Click the OK button

Notice in Figure 5-24 that I have set a Start No Earlier Than (SNET) constraint on Task B with a Constraint Date of 5/9/05.

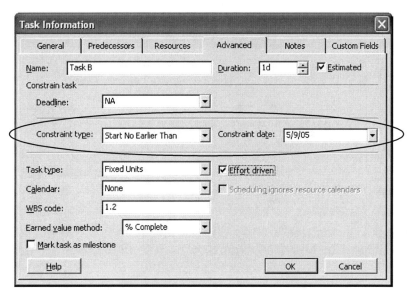

**Figure 5-24: Task Information Dialog Box
Advanced Page**

## Task Notes on Constraints

It is wise for you to add a Note when setting a constraint on a task. Adding a Note will make it easier for others to understand your reason for setting the constraint, and can be used later to understand the historical data in your project.

A good "shorthand" method for documenting a constraint is to include the following information in the text of the Note:

- Abbreviation for the constraint type (such as SNET)
- The date of the constraint (such as 05/09/05)
- The reason for setting the constraint

Figure 5-25 shows a Note documenting a constraint.

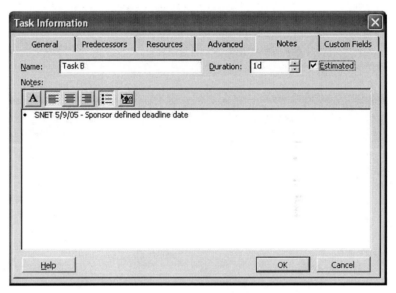

**Figure 5-25: Task Information dialog
Task Note documenting a constraint**

## Constraints: Flexible and Inflexible

In Microsoft Project 2003, constraints are either flexible or inflexible. A flexible constraint allows the software to behave as designed (to schedule). An Inflexible constraint limits (or even stops) the tool from behaving as designed.

Tables 5-1 and 5-2 document the behavior of Microsoft Project 2003 when you set a constraint in a project that is scheduled with a Start Date.

| Flexible Constraints | | |
|---|---|---|
| **Constraint Name** | **Color of Indicator** | **Constraint Description** |
| As Soon As Possible | None | Default constraint on new tasks when the project is scheduled with a start date |
| As Late As Possible | None | Default constraint on new tasks when the project is scheduled with a finish date |
| Start No Earlier Than | Blue | The task cannot start earlier than the constraint date |
| Finish No Earlier Than | Blue | The task cannot finish earlier than the constraint date |

**Table 5-1: Flexible Constraints**

| Inflexible Constraints | | |
|---|---|---|
| **Constraint Name** | **Color of Indicator** | **Constraint Description** |
| Must Start On | Red | The task must start on the constraint date |
| Must Finish On | Red | The task must finish on the constraint date |
| Start No Later Than | Red | The task cannot start later than the constraint date |
| Finish No Later Than | Red | The task cannot finish later than the constraint date |

**Table 5-2: Inflexible Constraints**

### *Planning Wizard Message Regarding Constraints*

When setting a task constraint in a project that is scheduled from a Start date, you will see a Planning Wizard message when two conditions are met:

- The constraint type is Inflexible (such as FNLT or MFO)
- The task is a successor to one or more predecessor tasks

The Planning Wizard message, such as the one shown in Figure 5-26, is a warning that these two conditions can cause potential scheduling problems in your project.

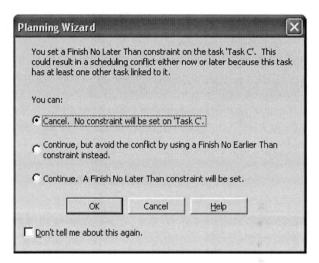

**Figure 5-26: Planning Wizard
message**

The default response in this dialog box is the first choice, which is to cancel the setting of the constraint. The Planning Wizard requires you to pick the third choice, Continue, if you truly want to set a constraint and risk potential scheduling problems.

# Setting Task Deadline Dates

In addition to Constraints, Microsoft Project 2003 allows you to set Deadline Dates as well. Deadline Dates are similar to Constraints, but do not limit the scheduling of the task on which a Deadline is added. When you set a Deadline date on a task, the software places a green arrow in the Gantt Chart to the right of the task's Gantt bar. If the task's Finish date moves beyond the deadline date, the software displays a special indicator in the Indicators column to show that the Deadline date was missed.

To set a Deadline date for any task, complete the following steps:

1. Double-click the task to which a Deadline date will be added

2. In the Task Information dialog box, shown in Figure 5-27, click the Advanced tab

3. Select a date from the Deadline drop-down list

4. Click the OK button

Notice in Figure 5-27 that I have set a Deadline Date of 11/4/05 on the PHASE I COMPLETE milestone task.

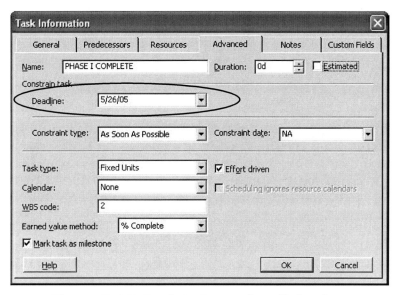

**Figure 5-27: Task Information dialog box
Set a Deadline date**

In Figure 5-28, the software shows the Deadline date with a hollow green arrow to the right of the task's Gantt bar in the Gantt Chart.

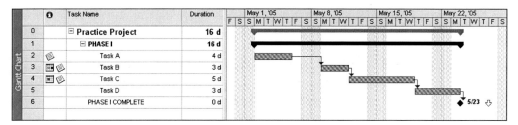

**Figure 5-28: Deadline date
indicator for Task C**

## *Missed Deadlines and Constraints*

Microsoft Project 2003 will give you limited warning when you have missed either a Deadline date or a Constraint date. When the Finish date of a task slips past its Deadline date, Microsoft Project 2003 will display a Missed Deadline indicator in the Indicators column to alert you to the missed Deadline date. Figure 5-29 shows a missed Deadline date with a warning indicator in the Indicators column.

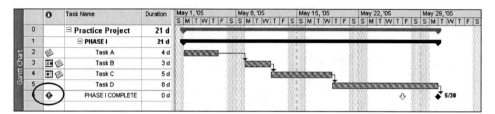

**Figure 5-29: Missed Deadline date**

When the Finish date of a task slips past an inflexible Constraint date, such as Finish No Later Than (FNLT) constraint, Microsoft Project 2003 displays a Planning Wizard dialog box, such as shown in Figure 5-30. In this dialog box, you will be warned of the slippage, and given an opportunity to either cancel the action that led to the slippage, or to allow the slippage to occur.

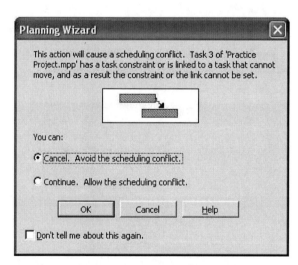

**Figure 5-30: Planning Wizard Message
Missed Constraint Date**

The default setting in this Planning Wizard dialog box is to cancel the action that is causing the slippage. If you select the second choice, Microsoft Project 2003 will complete the action and allow the scheduling conflict to exist in the project. Figure 5-31 shows a missed Constraint date on Task C, which has a Finish No Later Than (FNLT) constraint. Notice how the link line "bends back" between Tasks B and C, which is usually an indication of a missed constraint.

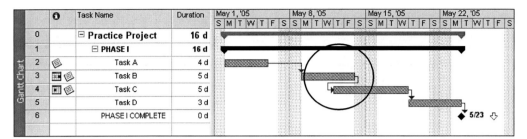

**Figure 5:31: Missed Constraint
date on Task B**

In Figure 5-31, Task B has finished late, which has caused Task C to slip to its Finish No Later Than (FNLT) constraint date on 5/18/05. This has caused a scheduling conflict because Microsoft Project 2003 will not allow Task C to slip past its inflexible Constraint date, as evidenced by the backward-bending link line between tasks B and C.

# Hands On Exercise

## Exercise 5-10

Now that task dependencies have been created in the Project Master Rollout project, you should set all necessary constraints and deadline dates. Several issues with this project will necessitate the use of constraints and Deadline dates, which are:

- Because of resource availability issues, the task Create Training Materials may not begin until March 1, 2007 or later

- In the Statement of Work, the finish date for the entire project has been set by contract as June 29, 2007

- The project manager has imposed on the project team an internal deadline date of June 15, 2007

In response to these issues, please apply two constraints and one Deadline date to tasks in the Project Master Rollout project.

1. **Create Training Materials**: Set a Start No Earlier Than constraint with a Constraint Date of 3/1/2007, and document the constraint with a bulleted Note that reads "SNET 3/1/07 - Resource availability date"

2. Zoom to Months over Weeks

3. **Project Complete**: Set a Must Finish On constraint with a Constraint Date of 6/29/07 and document the constraint with a bulleted Note that reads, "MFO 6/29/07 – Contractual deadline date for project"

4. When you see the Planning Wizard message about an inflexible Constraint, select the third choice (Continue) and then click the OK button

5. **Provide Training**: Set a Deadline date of 6/15/07

If the schedule of the Project Master Rollout project slips past the Deadline date of June 15, 2007, an indicator will appear in the Indicators column to warn of the slippage. If the schedule slips past the MFO constraint date on June 29, 2007, a Planning Wizard message will warn you that your project finish date is in jeopardy.

Your project should appear as is displayed in Figure 5-32.

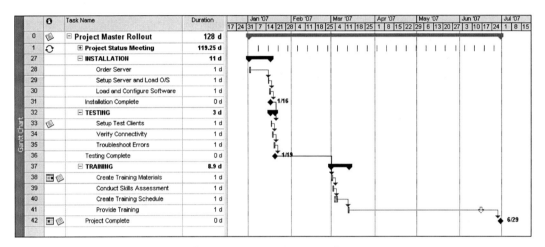

**Figure 5-32: Constraints
and Deadline date set**

6. Save and close your "Project Master05" project plan

# Module 06

## Project Planning – Resources

### Learning Objectives

After completing this module, you will be able to:

- Understand and use project resources
- Enter basic and custom resource information
- Understand how to create a Generic resource

# Defining Project Resources

Microsoft Project 2003 defines resources in a variety of ways and organizes them in the Project Resource Model as shown Figure 6-1.

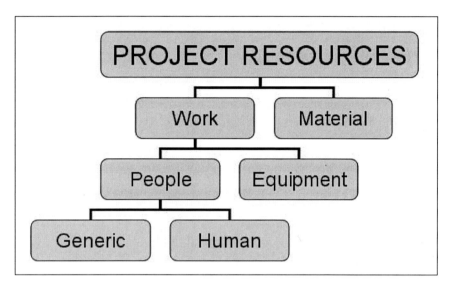

**Figure 6-1: Project Resource Model**

In Microsoft Project 2003, there are two basic types of resources: Work and Material. Work resources include people or equipment. Material resources represent the supplies consumed during the life of a project. Work resources affect both the schedule and the cost of the project, while Material resources affect only the project cost.

Microsoft Project 2003 organizes people resources into two groups: Generic and non-Generic (or Human Resources). A Human resource is a specific individual whom you can identify by name. A Generic resource is a skill-based placeholder resource, such as a C++ Software Developer. Generic resources allow you to specify the skills required for a task assignment before you know which Human resources are available to work on the task. You can later replace Generic resources with Human resources who possess the same skills.

It is important to identify all resources that you may eventually assign to tasks, and to enter the appropriate Unit availability for each resource into the Resource Sheet to show their availability for project work. The software measures the Unit availability of Work resources as a percentage, where 100% represents a full-time worker. The software also measures the Unit availability of Generic resources as a percentage; however, the percentage may exceed 100%. For example, to show that we have four full-time Software Developers available for project work, we would enter their Unit availability as 400%.

In Microsoft Project 2003, you cannot enter Unit availability for Material resources because Material resources affect only the cost and not the schedule of the project.

Prior to assigning resources to tasks, you should enter a variety of basic and custom resource information for each resource. Entering information such as the resource group, rate, accrual, calendar, and other pertinent information will allow you to:

- Track the amount of effort completed by work resources
- Track the amount of material resources consumed in completing tasks
- Be more accurate in scheduling how long tasks will take and when they are likely to be completed
- Monitor resources with too little or too much work assigned
- Manage resource time and costs

# Entering Basic Resource Information

The first step in defining resources is to enter basic resource information. The Resource Sheet view is ideal for entering this information. To view the Resource Sheet, click View ➤ Resource Sheet. Figure 6-2 shows the Resource Sheet view with the resource Entry table applied.

**Figure 6-2: Resource Sheet View
Entry Table applied**

Table 6-1 shows a description and recommended best uses for each of the default fields (columns) in the Resource Sheet view with the Entry table applied.

| Field | Description and Best Uses |
|---|---|
| ID | Calculated as you enter resources<br>Used by Microsoft Project 2003 when you assign resources to tasks |
| Indicators | Displays an icon for specific resource information such as resource Notes |
| Name | Used by Microsoft Project 2003 when you assign resources to tasks<br>Displayed in the Gantt Chart |
| Type | You can specify either Work or Material resources |
| Material Label | Defines the unit of measurement for the consumption of the Material resource |
| Initials | Can be displayed in the Gantt Chart |
| Group | Department or team identification<br>Can be used for filtering |
| Max Units | Measures the unit availability for the resource |
| Standard Rate | Project costing |
| Overtime Rate | Project costing |
| Cost/Use | Additional cost per task assignment |
| Accrue At | Apply actual costs at the Start, End, or on a Prorated basis for each task assignment |
| Base Calendar | The working and nonworking time schedule for each resource |
| Code | Department codes, accounting codes, cost center codes, etc.<br>Can be used for filtering |

**Table 6-1: Resource Sheet default fields**

To speed up the entry of resources, Microsoft Project 2003 allows you to fill data from one cell to consecutive cells above or below it. To do so, click and hold the Fill Handle in the lower right corner of the selected cell, and then drag as many cells as you would like filled.

# Entering Custom Resource Information

The second step in defining project resources is to enter custom resource information for each resource using the Resource Information dialog. To access this dialog, select a resource, and then use any of the following methods:

- Click Project ➤ Resource Information
- Double-click any cell in the row of the resource
- Click the Resource Information button on the Standard toolbar

 The Resource Information button on the Standard toolbar is the same button used to access Task Information in any Task view.

The Resource Information dialog includes five pages of information for each resource: the General, Working Time, Costs, Notes, and Custom Fields pages. Figure 6-3 shows the General page of the Resource Information dialog.

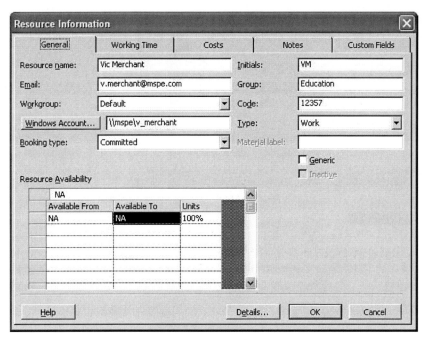

**Figure 6-3: Resource Information dialog
General page**

## General Page

The General page includes some information already entered in the Resource Sheet, such as Resource Name, Type, Initials, Group, and Code. It also allows you to enter additional information, such as the resource's Email address, method for receiving Workgroup messages, Windows user account, Resource Availability, and whether the resource is a Generic resource or an Inactive resource.

 To convert any resource from a Human resource to a Generic resource, select the Generic checkbox on the General page of the Resource Information dialog.

 The Resource Availability section is where you can enter changes in the availability of a resource over time, such as when a part-time employee becomes a full-time employee on a specific date. You can also use this section to indicate changes in the number of Generic resources available, for example, to show that our company will add two new network engineers on August 1.

msProjectExperts recommends that you always document changes in Resource Availability with a Note.

## Working Time Page

The Working Time page contains the resource's personal calendar, which is where you can enter the resource's non-working time, such as vacations and sick leave. You can also use the Working Time page to enter the resource's working schedule if it differs from the company's standard working schedule.

 msProjectExperts recommends that you document non-working time, such as vacations, with a Note. Doing so will make it easier to identify why Microsoft Project 2003 has scheduled any tasks to which the resource is assigned.

## Costs Page

The Costs page shows the Standard Rate, Overtime Rate, and Per Use Costs for the selected resource. In addition, this page also contains five Cost Rate tables labeled A through E. Cost Rate Table A normally contains the default rates for Standard, Overtime, and Per Use Cost. You can use Cost Rate Tables B through E for alternate cost rates. You can set any of these rates so that the rate changes on a given day.

 msProjectExperts recommends that you always document your use of Rate Tables with a Note. The Note should explain which Rate Table you are using and how you are using the alternate rate.

## Notes Page

You can use the Notes page to record additional text information about the selected resource, such as details about vacation and sick leave, changes in costs, and documentation about how the rates in the Rate Tables are used.

msProjectExperts recommends the use of resource Notes to document important resource information such as availability, vacations, and cost rates. Doing so will make it easier to understand how Microsoft Project 2003 calculates both the schedule and the cost of tasks to which the resource is assigned.

## Custom Fields Page

The Custom Fields page is to display any Enterprise resource fields specified in the Enterprise Global file. Many companies use the RBS (Resource Breakdown Structure) field to track the location of a resource in the company organization, and to use additional custom Enterprise fields to track other resource attributes such as skills and level of experience.

# Hands On Exercise

## Exercise 6-1

Enter the resources in the project team for the Project Master project.

1. Open the file called "Project Master06" from your student folder

2. At the bottom of the resource list, add two new resources using the information in Tables 6-2, 6-3, and 6-4

| Resource Name | Type | Material Label | Initials | Group |
|---|---|---|---|---|
| Training Developer | Work | | TD | TechEd |
| Vicky Joslyn | Work | | VJ | Test |

**Table 6-2**

| Resource Name | Max. Units | Std. Rate | Ovt. Rate | Cost/Use |
|---|---|---|---|---|
| Training Developer | 500% | $40.00/h | $60.00/h | $0.00 |
| Vicky Joslyn | 100% | $50.00/h | $75.00/h | $0.00 |

**Table 6-3**

| Resource Name | Accrue At | Base Calendar | Code |
|---|---|---|---|
| Training Developer | Prorated | msPE Standard | 401 |
| Vicky Joslyn | Prorated | msPE Standard | 500 |

**Table 6-4**

3. Make the Training Developer resource a Generic resource

## Exercise 6-2

Sort the resources in the Resource Sheet of Project Master. Apply a custom sort by the Type of resource, then by the resource's Group, and finally by the resource's name.

1. Click Project ➢ Sort ➢ Sort by to display the Sort dialog shown in Figure 6-4

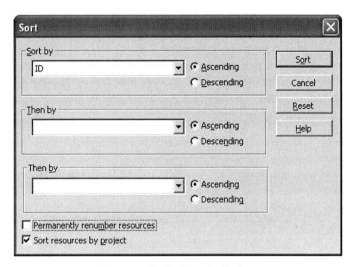

**Figure 6-4: Sort dialog**

2. In the Sort by field, select Type and then select the Descending option

3. In the first Then by field, select Group

4. In the second Then by field, select Name

5. Select the Permanently renumber resources option

6. Click the Sort button

 If you want to sort the Resource Sheet in alphabetical order by last name then first name, two methods you can use are:

- Type the names in reverse order in the Name field without using a comma

- Type the names with commas in a custom Text field and then alphabetize using the contents of the Text field

## Exercise 6-3

Enter custom resource information for selected members of the project team in Project Master.

1. Modify the calendar for Mickey Cobb and set February 5-9, 2007 as nonworking time

2. Document the reason for Mickey's Cobb's nonworking time as vacation by adding a resource Note

3. Modify the calendar for Jeff Holly and set March 12-16, 2007 as nonworking time

4. Document the reason for Jeff Holly's nonworking time as medical leave (surgery) by adding a resource Note

Figures 6-5 and 6-6 show the Resource Information dialog for Jeff Holly.

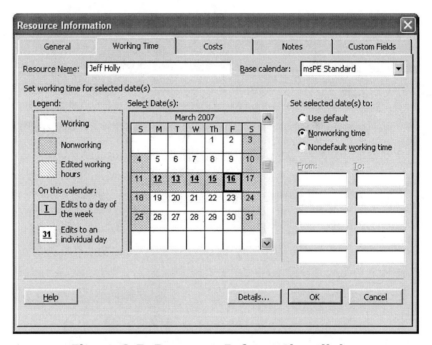

**Figure 6-5: Resource Information dialog
Working Time page with nonworking time**

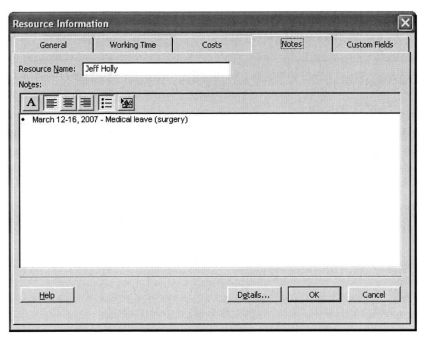

**Figure 6-6: Resource Information dialog**
**Notes page to document nonworking time**

5. Apply a 10% increase to the standard and overtime cost rates for Carolyn Fross, effective April 1, 2007

Figure 6-7 shows the Costs page of the Resource Information dialog for Carolyn Fross.

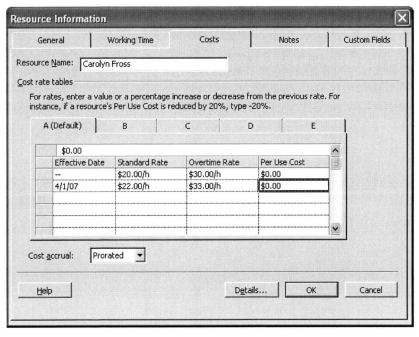

**Figure 6-7: Resource Information dialog**
**Costs page with rate increase**

Mike Andrews works on the Help Desk, but does occasional testing work billed at the same rate as members of Test team.

6.  For Mike Andrews, add an alternate Cost rate of $50.00/hr for the Standard Rate and $75.00/hr for the Overtime Rate on Cost Rate Table B

7.  Document the reason for the alternate rate using a resource Note

Figure 6-8 shows the resource Cost page for Mike Andrews.

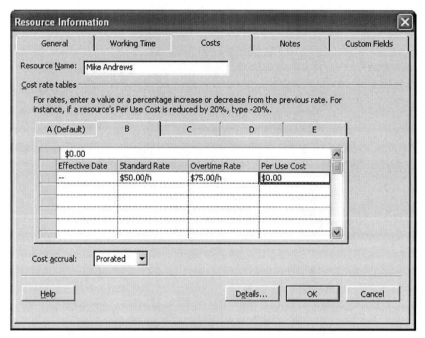

**Figure 6-8: Resource Information dialog
Cost Rate Table B on the Costs page**

8.  Save and close your "Project Master06" project plan

# Module 07

## Project Planning - Assignments

### Learning Objectives

After completing this module, you will be able to:

- Understand resource capabilities and work estimating
- Assign resources to tasks
- Understand Task Types and Effort-Driven Scheduling

# Task and Resource Assignments

Now that you have defined tasks and resources, you are ready to make assignments. When you assign a resource to a task, the Microsoft Project 2003 creates an assignment in the Microsoft Project Data Model, as shown in Figure 7-1.

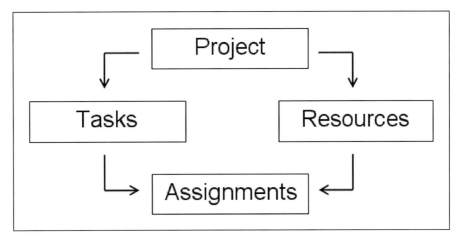

**Figure 7-1: Microsoft Project
Data Model completed**

## *Identifying Resource Capabilities*

You should assign resources carefully, making sure that the resources possess the knowledge, skills, and abilities required to complete the task within the allotted time and budget. If you have any doubt about the capabilities of the resource, you should arrange for training or mentoring to eliminate any skill deficiencies. Remember: skill deficiencies are risks to projects, and like any other risk, you must have contingency plans in place.

## *Estimating Task Effort*

In addition to identifying resource capabilities, you must estimate task effort as well. Determining the appropriate level of effort can be challenging, especially if the task is unique or the skills of the resource are questionable.

Some companies use specific methodologies for estimating task effort. A good example is the "5 and 80" methodology which states that tasks should have no less than 5 hours of effort and no more than 80 hours of effort. Some companies use a "4 and 40" methodology so that tasks with less than 4 hours of effort are merged with others, while tasks with more than 40 hours of effort are split into multiple tasks.

### *Resource Assignments: A Best Practice*

The Project Management Institute (PMI) recommends that as often as possible, you should involve resources in the estimating process, or you should at least allow them to approve the estimate since they perform the work. Their estimates may be more accurate, and involving resources in the estimating process instills a sense of project ownership. During the execution stage of the project, this sense of ownership by team members becomes invaluable when they begin reporting actual progress on their task work.

# Assigning Resources in the Task Entry View

Once you have identified the resources required and have estimated their effort, you can set the resources, Units, and Work (effort) in the Microsoft Project 2003 plan. The Task Entry view is the recommended location for assigning resources and effort to tasks. To apply the Task Entry view, complete the following steps:

1. Click View ➢ More Views

2. Scroll to and select Task Entry, and then click Apply

 The fastest way to display the Task Entry view is to double-click the horizontal split bar indicator at the bottom of the vertical scroll bar. Your can also drag the split bar and manually resize the top and bottom panes in the Task Entry view.

The Task Entry view is a combination view consisting of the Gantt Chart view in the top pane, and the Task Form view in the bottom pane as displayed in Figure 7-2.

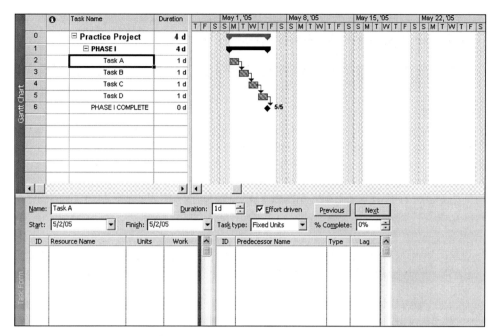

**Figure 7-2: Task Entry View**

You will find many advantages using the Task Entry view for making resource assignments, including:

- It is the recommended view for the YJTJ process (Your Job, Tool's Job).

- All of the primary components of the software's scheduling engine are accessible including: Resource Name, Units, Work, Duration, Task Types, and Effort Driven scheduling.

- When you change the Units, Work, or Duration value on any task, you can easily determine the effect on the project schedule.

The only disadvantage of using the Task Entry view is that you cannot assign resources to multiple tasks simultaneously.

# Hands On Exercise

## Exercise 7-1

**Installation:** Assign resources to the tasks in the INSTALLATION phase of the Project Master project.

1. Open the file called "Project Master07" from your student folder

2. Zoom to Weeks Over Days

3. Select the task Order Server and then click the Go To Selected Task button on the Standard toolbar

4. Apply the Task Entry view

5. In the Task Form, assign Mickey Cobb to the task Order Server at 75% Units and 12 hours of Work, and then click the OK button

6. In the Task Form, click the Next button to select the task Setup Server and Load O/S

7. Assign Jeff Holly to the task Setup Server and Load O/S at 80% Units and 32 hours of Work

8. Assign Carmen Kamper to the task Load and Configure Software at 70% Units and 44 hours of Work

Your project should appear as is shown in Figure 7-3.

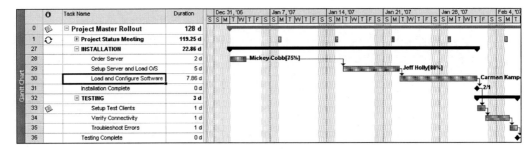

**Figure 7-3: INSTALLATION assignments completed**

**Testing:** Assign resources to deliverable tasks in the TESTING phase of the Project Master project.

1. Roll up the INSTALLATION summary task

2. Select the task Setup Test Clients and then click the Go To Selected Task button on the Standard toolbar

3. Assign Dave Harbaugh to the task Setup Test Clients at 40% Units and 50 hours of Work

4. Assign Mike Andrews to the task Verify Connectivity at 60% Units and 55 hours of Work

5. Assign Bob Jared to the task Troubleshoot Errors at 50% Units and 80 hours of Work

6. Select anywhere in the upper pane and then Zoom to Months over Weeks

Your Project Master project should appear as is shown in Figure 7-4.

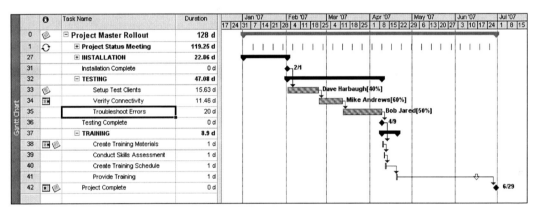

**Figure 7-4: TESTING assignments completed**

**Training:** Assign resources to deliverable tasks in the TRAINING phase of the Project Master project.

1. Roll up the TESTING summary task

2. Select the task Create Training Materials and then click the Go To Selected Task button on the Standard toolbar

3. Assign the Training Developer to the task Create Training Materials at 100% Units and 120 hours of Work

4. Assign Chuck Kirkpatrick and Kent Bergstrand to the task Conduct Skills Assessment at 50% Units each and 40 hours of Work each

5. Assign Kent Bergstrand to the task Create Training Schedule at 50% Units and 24 hours of Work

When the training materials are complete and the training schedule has been set, the company will offer three sets of concurrent training classes at three different locations on the company campus.

6. Assign Chuck Kirkpatrick, Kent Bergstrand, and Ruth Andrews to the task Provide Training at 100% Units and 80 hours of Work each

Your Project Master project should appear as is shown in Figure 7-5.

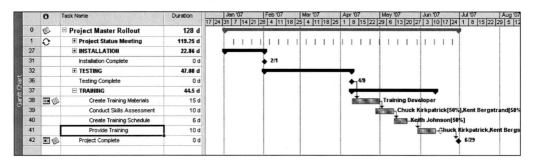

**Figure 7-5: TRAINING assignments completed**

7. Roll out the TESTING and the INSTALLATION summary tasks

8. Save but do not close your "Project Master07" project

# The Duration Equation

When you assign a resource to a task using the Task Entry view, you supply the resource's Name, plus Units and Work hours (Your Job). Microsoft Project 2003 then calculates the Duration (Tool's Job). How does it calculate Duration? The software uses a simple formula known as the Duration Equation, which is:

**D**uration = **W**ork ÷ (**P**roject **H**ours **P**er **D**ay × **U**nits)

You can abbreviate this equation as follows:

D = W ÷ (PHPD × U)

The PHPD value is usually 8 hours per day. You can find this value on the Calendar page of the project Options dialog by clicking Tools ➢ Options, and then clicking the Calendar tab, as shown in Figure 7-6.

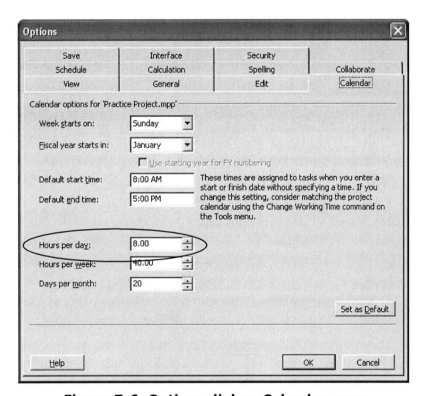

**Figure 7-6: Options dialog, Calendar page
Hours per Day setting**

To see how the Duration Equation works, assume that you have assigned Sarah Baker to Task A at 50% Units and 40 hours of Work. The Duration Equation would calculate the Duration as 10 days, as follows:

D = W ÷ (PHPD × U)
D = 40 ÷ (8 × 50%)
D = 40 ÷ 4 = 10 days

Figure 7-7 shows the Units, Work, and Duration variables in the Duration Equation in the Task Form portion of the Task Entry view.

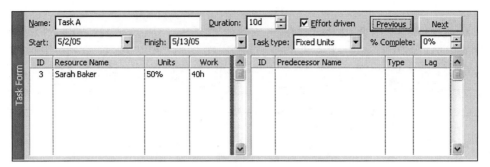

**Figure 7-7: Task Form shows
Duration Equation values**

## *Microsoft Project "Task Types"*

In the scheduling engine of Microsoft Project 2003, you can to fix or "lock" one of the three variables in the Duration Equation. This prevents the software from recalculating the fixed variable when you know the value of that variable with certainty.

In Microsoft Project 2003, you will set the Task Type value to lock one of the three variables. You can see the Task Type value in the Task Form as shown previously in Figure 7-7. The three Task Types are Fixed Units (the default), Fixed Work, and Fixed Duration.

- **Fixed Units** – The software locks the Units value for all resources assigned to a Fixed Units task. Set the Task Type to Fixed Units when a resource has a known availability to perform work on tasks in your project.

- **Fixed Work** – The software locks the Work value for all resources assigned to a Fixed Work task. Use this Task Type when you are confident about the number of hours to complete a task, such as when you have agreed to the number of hours of work by contract.

- **Fixed Duration** – The software locks the Duration value of the task on a Fixed Duration task. Use this Task Type when you are confident of the Duration of a task, such as when you have a known "window of opportunity" to complete the task.

# Assigning Resources in the Assign Resources Dialog

The Assign Resources dialog is a quick and easy way to assign resources to tasks. However, it is best used for assigning resources to Recurring Tasks (such as meetings), or for substituting human resources for Generic resources. To access this dialog, use either of the following methods:

1. Click Tools ➢ Assign Resources

2. Click the Assign Resources button on the Standard toolbar

Figure 7-8 shows the initial view of the Assign Resources dialog.

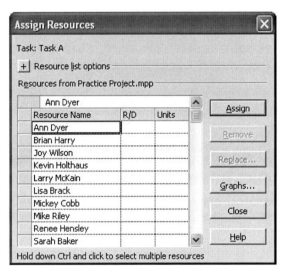

**Figure 7-8: Assign Resources dialog**
**Resource list options hidden**

The Assign Resources dialog is ideal for assigning resources to Recurring Tasks, such as meetings, as it allows you to select and assign multiple resources to a task. This dialog is also ideal for replacing Generic Resources with Human Resources when you have already defined Work, Duration, and Effort Driven. The primary disadvantage of this dialog is that you cannot access the components in scheduling engine, such as Work, Duration, Task Types, or Effort Driven.

 In the Assign Resources dialog, the software sorts the resources in ascending order by Resource Name, and not in the order that they appear on the Resource Sheet view.

# Hands On Exercise

## Exercise 7-2

Assign resources to a recurring task in the Project Master project using the Assign Resources dialog.

1. Make sure that the "Project Master07" file is open with the Task Entry view applied

2. In the upper pane, select the Project Status Meeting recurring task

3. Click the Assign Resources button on the Standard toolbar

4. Use the Control key to select the following resources simultaneously and then click the Assign button:

   - Carolyn Fross – administrative assistant

   - Helen Howard – NetOps team leader

   - Melena Keeth – TechEd team leader

   - Richard Sanders – project manager

   - Vicky Joslyn – Test team leader

5. Click the Close button to close the Assign Resources dialog

6. Roll out the occurrences of the Project Status Meeting recurring task

7. Select the Status Meeting 1 occurrence in the upper viewing pane

Notice in the lower viewing pane that the software has assigned each resource at 100% Units and 2 hours of Work for this meeting.

8. Save but do not close your "Project Master07" project

# Assigning Material Resources to a Task

You can assign Material resources to a task using either of two methods. You can assign a Material resource at a *fixed consumption* rate when the amount of the resource consumed does not depend upon the Duration of the task. For example, when you assign the resource Paper at "25 Reams" to a Project Administration task, 25 reams of paper will be consumed regardless of the duration of the task.

You can assign a Material resource at a *variable consumption* rate when the amount of the resource consumed is directly dependent on the Duration of the task. For example, when you assign the resource Gasoline to the task Excavate Site at 100 gallons/day, 500 gallons will be consumed in 5 days, 800 gallons will be consumed in 8 days, etc. When assigning a Material resource to a task, make sure that you pick the correct method of assignment.

# Hands On Exercise

## Exercise 7-3

Assign a Material resource to a task in the Project Master project.

1. Make sure that the "Project Master07" file is open with the Task Entry view applied

2. In the upper viewing pane, select the Project Status Meetings recurring task

3. Click the Assign Resources button again on the Standard toolbar

4. Select the Paper resource and type the number "1" in the Units column

5. Click the Assign button

6. Click the Close button to close the Assign Resources dialog

7. Select the Status Meeting 1 occurrence in the upper viewing pane

Notice in the lower viewing pane that one ream of Paper has been assigned for this (and every) meeting, as shown in Figure 7-9.

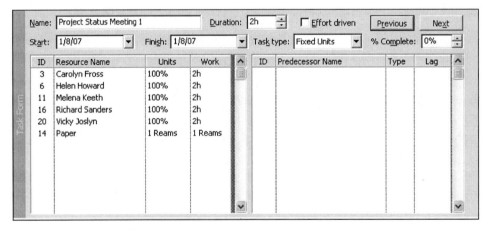

**Figure 7-9: Resource assignments
on Project Status Meeting 1**

8. Roll up the Project Status Meeting occurrences

9. Save but do not close your "Project Master07" project

# Using Effort Driven Scheduling

You will normally use effort-driven scheduling to shorten the Duration of a task by adding additional resources to the task. Effort-driven scheduling keeps the total Remaining Work constant on the task while you add or remove resources.

For example, a 40-hour task with one resource assigned at 100% units yields a Duration of 5 days for the task. Using effort-driven scheduling, adding a second resource at 100% units shortens the Duration to 2.5 days and evenly reallocates the 40 hours of Remaining Work between the two resources.

 On Fixed Units or Fixed Work tasks, adding additional resources will shorten the Duration of the task. On a Fixed Duration task, adding additional resources will decrease the Units for each resource.

# Hands On Exercise

## Exercise 7-4

After reviewing the project schedule, Senior Management has made a decision to shorten the duration of the task by assigning an additional resource to assist with the work. Therefore, use effort-driven scheduling to shorten the Duration of this task.

1. Select the task Troubleshoot Errors and click the Go To Selected Task button on the Standard toolbar

2. Add the resource Terry Uland to the task Troubleshoot Errors at 50% Units (do not type a Work value) and click OK

3. Change the 40 hours of work for each resource assigned to the task Setup Test Clients to 48 hours and click OK

> msProjectExperts recommends that when adding resources to a task using effort-driven scheduling, you should increase the Work hours for each resource in the range of 10% to 20% to account for the increased communications needs between the resources.

Figure 7-10 displays the result of assigning an additional resource to an effort-driven task.

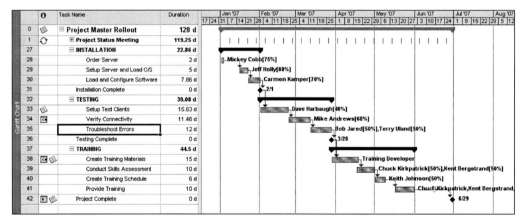

**Figure 7-10: Assignment using
Effort-Driven scheduling**

4. Close the lower viewing pane to return to a single pane Gantt Chart view

5. Save but do not close your "Project Master07" project

# Using Resource Substitution

When using Generic or skill-based resources, you will eventually need to substitute a Human resource for one or more Generic resources. You can accomplish this using the Assign Resources dialog. This dialog contains a number of helpful options that can be accessed by clicking the Resource List Options button at the top of the dialog. Figure 7-11 shows the Assign Resources dialog with the Resource List Options expanded.

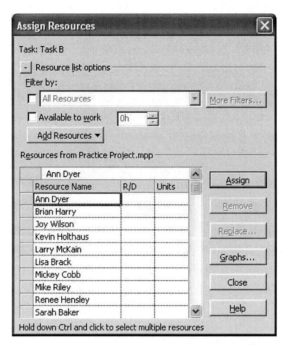

**Figure 7-11: Assign Resources dialog
Resource List Options displayed**

The Resource list options allow you to apply a Filter, such as the Group filter, to locate a Human resource with the right skills, as is displayed in Figure 7-12.

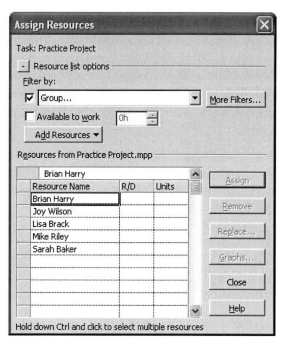

**Figure 7-12: Assign Resources dialog
Group filter applied**

After a Filter has been applied, you can also locate a Human resource with the necessary availability during a specified time period. To do so, select the Available to work option and set a value such as 40 hours, as is displayed in Figure 7-13.

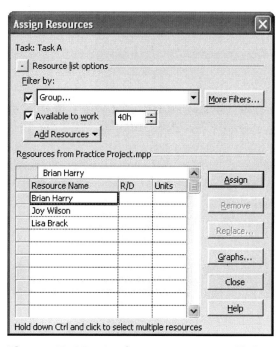

**Figure 7-13: Assign Resources dialog
Available to Work 40 hours**

Notice that two resources, Mike Riley and Sarah Baker, dropped off the list of available resources when the project manager searched for resources with at least 40 hours of availability. This means that these two resources are assigned to another task during the same time period and would not be available to work on Task A.

In addition, once you have located any Human resources with the right skills and necessary availability, a resource graph can be displayed by clicking the Graphs button in the Assign Resources dialog. Figure 7-14 shows how the Resource Graph can be used to determine how much Work the resource Sarah Baker is assigned during the months of May and June 2005.

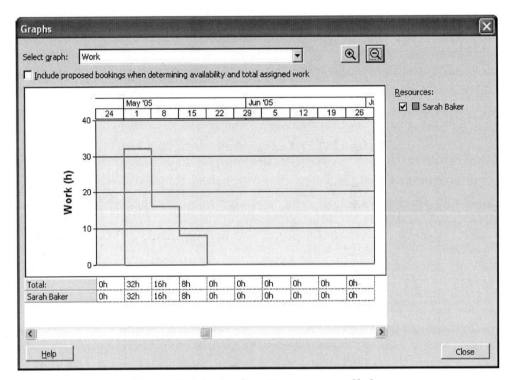

**Figure 7-14: Assign Resources dialog
Graphs page for Phyllis Dyer**

From the graph shown in Figure 7-14, we can see that Sarah is assigned to 32 hours of work during the week of 5/1/05, to 16 hours of work during the week of 5/8/05, and to 8 hours of work during the week of 5/15/05. Thus, she should be unable to work full-time on another task during the same three-week time span.

# Hands On Exercise

## Exercise 7-5

Locate and substitute an available human resource for the Generic resource assigned to the Project Master project.

1. Select the task Create Training Materials and then click the Assign Resources button on the Standard toolbar

2. Click the outline symbol (the + button) in front of the Resource list options section to display additional options for assigning resources

3. Select the Filter by checkbox and select the Group filter

4. In the Group dialog, type TechEd as the Group name, and then click the OK button

5. Select the Available to work checkbox and set the field to 120 hours

When you set the Available to work option to 120 hours, this will guarantee that the filtered resource list contains only those resources that are available to work on this task. Notice that Marilyn Ray and Ruth Andrews are the only resources with both the skills *and* the 120 hours of availability to work on this task.

6. Select the Generic resource, Training Developer, and click the Replace button

7. In the Replace Resource dialog, select Ruth Andrews and then click the OK button

8. Click the Close button to close the Assign resources dialog

9. Save and close your "Project Master07" project plan

# More about the Assign Resources Dialog

In an enterprise environment using Project Server 2003, there are several additional options in the Assign Resources dialog. You can add additional resources to a project by clicking the Add Resources drop-down button. You can add resources from an Active Directory, from a corporate Address Book, or from the Project Server's Enterprise Resource Pool, as is displayed in Figure 7-15.

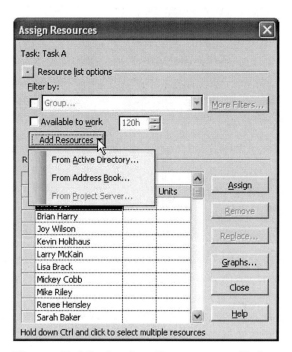

**Figure 7-15: Assign Resources dialog
Add Resources choices**

The Assign Resources dialog also allows you to set an assigned resource as either a Request resource or a Demand resource in the R/D column of the dialog. You would use this feature in conjunction with the Resource Substitution Wizard. The R/D value you set specifies whether the assigned resource must perform the task (Demand) or whether any qualified resource may perform the task (Request). Figure 7-16 shows the R/D options in the Assign Resources dialog.

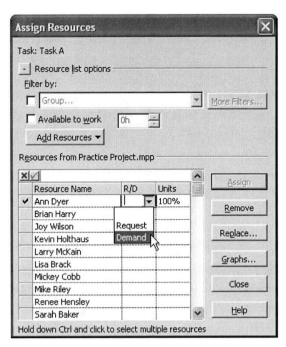

**Figure 7-16: Assign Resources dialog
Request/Demand option**

Building a team from the Enterprise Resource Pool and using the Resource Substitution Wizard are both discussed in the Microsoft Project Server 2003 for Project Managers course from msProjectExperts.

# Module 08

## Project Execution

### Learning Objectives

After completing this module, you will be able to:

- Save an original baseline for a project
- Understand the proper use of the multiple Baseline fields in Microsoft Project 2003
- Understand the three primary methods for entering project progress
- Use a "Best Practice" for entering project progress using the timesheet method

# Project Execution Defined

Project execution is the process of moving forward with the project plan. During execution, you will save a project baseline, track project progress, analyze project variance, revise the project, manage project change, and report project progress.

## *What is a Baseline?*

Prior to executing a project, you must save a baseline for your project. A baseline represents your "best guesstimate" about the schedule of the project. The project baseline will also provide you the means for doing variance analysis, plan revision, change control, and reporting project progress.

When you save a Baseline for a project in Microsoft Project 2003, the software saves the current state of five values for each task, along with the current state of two values for each resource. The values saved for each task in a project Baseline are:

- Duration
- Start
- Finish
- Work
- Cost

The values saved for each resource in a project Baseline are:

- Work
- Cost

# Saving a Project Baseline

To save a baseline for the entire project in Microsoft Project 2003, complete the following steps:

1. Click Tools ➤ Tracking ➤ Save Baseline

2. Select the Save Baseline option and select Baseline from the drop-down list of baseline fields

3. In the For: section, select the Entire project option and then click the OK button

Figure 8-1 shows the Save Baseline dialog.

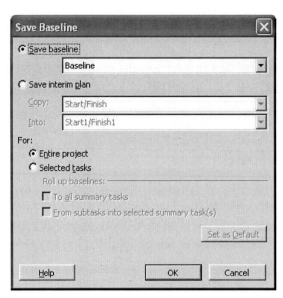

**Figure 8-1: Save Baseline**
**dialog**

 In addition to saving a Baseline for the entire project, you can save a Baseline for selected tasks only. You also have the option of saving your Baseline in the original Baseline field, or in one of ten additional Baseline fields (Baseline 1 through Baseline10).

 msProjectExperts recommends that you save an original baseline only once during the life of the project. After a change control procedure that adds new tasks to your project, you may save a Baseline for only the new tasks. This will maintain the integrity of your original project baseline.

Should you attempt to resave your Baseline later, Microsoft Project 2003 will show you that have already saved a Baseline and the date on which you saved the Baseline, as displayed in Figure 8-2.

**Figure 8-2: Save Baseline dialog**
**Date of baseline save**

If you continue the process of saving your new baseline over the original Baseline field, Microsoft Project 2003 will warn you with the dialog shown in Figure 8-3.

**Figure 8-3: Warning dialog**
**Overwrite original baseline**

## *Viewing the Project Baseline*

When you save a baseline for our project, the process does not actually "save" the project file. Rather, while saving a Baseline, Microsoft Project 2003 simply copies the current values from one set of fields to the Baseline set of fields. For example, the software copies current value from the Work field to the Baseline Work field for each task when you save a Baseline. You can view the five types of baseline data for each task by completing the following steps:

1. Display any task view, such as the Gantt Chart or Task Sheet view

2. Right-click the Select All button and select More Tables

3. Select the Baseline table and click the Apply button

Figure 8-4 shows the task Baseline table.

| | Task Name | Baseline Dur. | Baseline Start | Baseline Finish | Baseline Work | Baseline Cost |
|---|---|---|---|---|---|---|
| 0 | ⊟ **Sample Project** | **22 d** | **5/2/05** | **5/31/05** | **184 h** | **$11,040.00** |
| 1 | ⊟ **PHASE I** | **22 d** | **5/2/05** | **5/31/05** | **184 h** | **$11,040.00** |
| 2 | Task A | 5 d | 5/2/05 | 5/6/05 | 40 h | $2,400.00 |
| 3 | Task B | 4 d | 5/9/05 | 5/12/05 | 24 h | $2,400.00 |
| 4 | Task C | 2 d | 5/13/05 | 5/16/05 | 16 h | $800.00 |
| 5 | Task D | 5 d | 5/17/05 | 5/23/05 | 80 h | $4,000.00 |
| 6 | Task E | 6 d | 5/24/05 | 5/31/05 | 24 h | $1,440.00 |
| 7 | PHASE I COMPLETE | 0 d | 5/31/05 | 5/31/05 | 0 h | $0.00 |

**Figure 8-4: Gantt Chart view**
**Baseline table applied**

To view baseline information for resources, display the Resource Sheet view, with the Entry table applied, and then temporarily insert the Baseline Work and Baseline Cost fields.

After you have baselined your project, you should also save your project as well.

## *Clearing the Project Baseline*

Sometime you may prematurely save the Baseline for a project, such as when a management decision delays the start of your project for any reason. In situations like this, your Baseline will be invalid once a new project start date is set. Therefore, you may want to clear the baseline for your project by completing the following steps:

1. Click Tools ➤ Tracking Clear ➤ Baseline

2. Select the Clear baseline plan option and select Baseline from the drop-down list of baseline fields

3. In the For: section, make sure the Entire project option is selected, then click the OK button

Figure 8-5 shows the Clear Baseline dialog.

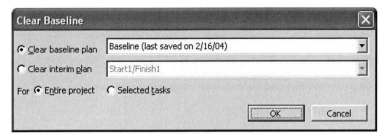

**Figure 8-5: Clear Baseline dialog**

 You can also clear the Baseline for selected tasks only, as well as for the entire project. In Project 2003, you have the option of clearing your Baseline from the original Baseline field, or from one of ten additional Baseline fields (Baseline 1 through Baseline10).

# Hands On Exercise

## Exercise 8-1

Now that you have finished project planning, you are ready to save a baseline for the Project Master project.

1. Open the file called "Project Master08" from your student folder

2. Right-click the Select All button and select More Tables

3. Select the Baseline table and click the Apply button

4. "Best Fit" the Task Name column, if necessary

5. Pull the vertical split bar all the way to the right so that you can see all of the Baseline columns

6. Save a baseline in the Baseline field for the entire project

Figure 8-6 shows the Baseline table for the Project Master project.

| | | Task Name | Baseline Dur. | Baseline Start | Baseline Finish | Baseline Work | Baseline Cost |
|---|---|---|---|---|---|---|---|
| | 0 | ⊟ **Project Master Rollout** | **128 d** | **1/2/07** | **6/29/07** | **1,003 h** | **$43,087.00** |
| | 1 | ⊞ **Project Status Meeting** | **119.25 d** | **1/8/07** | **6/25/07** | **250 h** | **$11,177.00** |
| | 27 | ⊟ **INSTALLATION** | **22.86 d** | **1/2/07** | **2/1/07** | **88 h** | **$4,400.00** |
| | 28 | Order Server | 2 d | 1/2/07 | 1/3/07 | 12 h | $600.00 |
| | 29 | Setup Server and Load O/S | 5 d | 1/16/07 | 1/22/07 | 32 h | $1,600.00 |
| | 30 | Load and Configure Software | 7.86 d | 1/23/07 | 2/1/07 | 44 h | $2,200.00 |
| | 31 | Installation Complete | 0 d | 2/1/07 | 2/1/07 | 0 h | $0.00 |
| | 32 | ⊟ **TESTING** | **39.08 d** | **2/1/07** | **3/28/07** | **201 h** | **$8,950.00** |
| | 33 | Setup Test Clients | 15.63 d | 2/1/07 | 2/23/07 | 50 h | $2,500.00 |
| | 34 | Verify Connectivity | 11.46 d | 2/23/07 | 3/12/07 | 55 h | $1,650.00 |
| | 35 | Troubleshoot Errors | 12 d | 3/12/07 | 3/28/07 | 96 h | $4,800.00 |
| | 36 | Testing Complete | 0 d | 3/28/07 | 3/28/07 | 0 h | $0.00 |
| | 37 | ⊟ **TRAINING** | **44.5 d** | **3/28/07** | **5/31/07** | **464 h** | **$18,560.00** |
| | 38 | Create Training Materials | 15 d | 3/28/07 | 4/18/07 | 120 h | $4,800.00 |
| | 39 | Conduct Skills Assessment | 10 d | 4/17/07 | 5/1/07 | 80 h | $3,200.00 |
| | 40 | Create Training Schedule | 6 d | 5/1/07 | 5/9/07 | 24 h | $960.00 |
| | 41 | Provide Training | 10 d | 5/16/07 | 5/31/07 | 240 h | $9,600.00 |
| | 42 | Project Complete | 0 d | 6/29/07 | 6/29/07 | 0 h | $0.00 |

**Figure 8-6: Baseline Table**

7. Reapply the Entry table, then pull the vertical split bar back to the right edge of the Duration column

8. Save and close your "Project Master08" file

# Tracking Project Progress

Once the project is underway, the next step in project execution is to begin collecting actual project data from your team members in order to track project progress. You must make it very clear to project team members as to the importance of tracking actual data. Collecting actual project data is the first step toward a clear understanding of the current state of the project.

There are three general methods for tracking project progress in Microsoft Project 2003. These methods are follows:

- % Complete
- Actual Work + Remaining Work
- Daily Timesheet + Remaining Work

Each of these methods for tracking project progress offers both advantages and disadvantages.

## *Entering % Complete*

The simplest method of tracking progress is to ask your team members to estimate the percentage of the work that they have completed on each task during the reporting period. This method works well for construction projects, where you can accurately measure the physical amount of work completed. This method is much less reliable in other environments, such as with software development projects.

The chief limitation of the % Complete method of tracking is that it is not date-sensitive. In fact, when you enter a % Complete value for a task in Microsoft Project 2003, the software assumes that the task started and finished *as scheduled*.

If you wish to use the % Complete method for tracking project progress, you can address this date limitation by gathering the following progress information from each team member for each task assignment:

- Actual Start Date
- % Complete
- Actual Finish Date

During each reporting period, your team members should report the actual date they began work on a task, along with their estimate of the percentage of work completed on the task. When the task is completed, your team members will report the actual date that the work was completed.

To enter the Actual Start date, % Complete, and Actual Finish date in Microsoft Project 2003, complete the following steps:

1. Apply the Gantt Chart view

2. Right-click on the Select All button and select the Tracking table

3. "Best Fit" the Task Name column, if necessary

4. Pull the vertical split bar to the right of the % Complete field

5. "Drag and drop" the % Complete field between the Actual Start and Actual Finish fields

6. Enter the actual start date of each resource assignment in the Actual Start column

7. Enter an estimated % complete in the % Complete field

8. When the task is completed, enter the completion date in the Actual Finish field

Figure 8-7 shows the Tracking table set up for entry of project progress using the % Complete method. Notice that Task A is 100% complete with both an Actual Start and Actual Finish date. Task B is only 50% complete with an Actual Start date and with no Actual Finish date.

| | | Task Name | Act. Start | % Comp. | Act. Finish | Phys. % Comp. | Act. Dur. | Rem. Dur. | Act. Cost | Act. Work |
|---|---|---|---|---|---|---|---|---|---|---|
| | 0 | ⊟ **Sample Project** | **5/2/05** | **32%** | **NA** | **0%** | **7.32 d** | **15.68 d** | **$3,600.00** | **52 h** |
| | 1 | ⊟ **PHASE I** | **5/2/05** | **32%** | **NA** | **0%** | **7.32 d** | **15.68 d** | **$3,600.00** | **52 h** |
| | 2 | Task A | 5/2/05 | 100% | 5/6/05 | 0% | 5 d | 0 d | $2,400.00 | 40 h |
| | 3 | Task B | 5/10/05 | 50% | NA | 0% | 2 d | 2 d | $1,200.00 | 12 h |
| | 4 | Task C | NA | 0% | NA | 0% | 0 d | 2 d | $0.00 | 0 h |
| | 5 | Task D | NA | 0% | NA | 0% | 0 d | 5 d | $0.00 | 0 h |
| | 6 | Task E | NA | 0% | NA | 0% | 0 d | 6 d | $0.00 | 0 h |
| | 7 | PHASE I COMPLETE | NA | 0% | NA | 0% | 0 d | 0 d | $0.00 | 0 h |

**Figure 8-7: Tracking table set up
for entry of % Complete**

In Figure 8-7, Task B actually started one day late against its Baseline Start date. In a situation such as this, msProjectExperts recommends that you use a task Note to document the late start or late finish of a task. Using task Notes will provide accurate project documentation on schedule problems during the execution of the project, and may assist with better date estimation on future projects.

**Hands On Exercise**

## Exercise 8-2

Enter project progress using the % Complete method in the Project Master project.

1. Open the file called "Project Master08a" from your student folder

2. Apply the Tracking table and set it up for entry of actual progress using the % Complete method

3. Enter an Actual Start date of 01/02/07 for the task Order Server

4. Enter an Actual Finish date of 01/03/07 for the task Order Server

Notice that the task is marked as 100% Complete automatically.

5. Enter an Actual Start date of 01/18/07 for the task Setup Server and Load O/S

Notice that the Gantt bar for this task moved two days later.

6. Enter a % Complete of 25% for the task Setup Server and Load O/S

The delivery of the new server was two days late, therefore, this task is two days behind schedule. Furthermore, Jeff Holly is also behind schedule since he completed only 25% of the work on this task. Because the task is not yet complete, you will not enter an Actual Finish date.

7. Save and close "Project Master08a"

## *Entering Actual Work and Remaining Work*

Another method of tracking project progress is to ask team members to record their total actual work hours during each reporting period, and to provide their estimate on the amount of remaining work for each task. For example, a designer reports 20 hours of Actual Work on a 40-hour task, and adjusts the Remaining Work estimate from 20 hours to 30 hours because he needs to redo some of the work.

This method will allow you to see date slippage, based on the revised Remaining Work estimates submitted by your team members. However, this method may not present a true picture of task progress, especially if a task started late. When using this method for tracking project progress, Microsoft Project 2003 will once again assume that each task started *as scheduled* and will calculate when the task actually finished.

If you wish to use the Actual Work and Remaining Work method for tracking project progress, you can address the date limitation issue by the following progress information from each team member for each task assignment:

- Actual Start Date
- Actual Work and Remaining Work
- Actual Finish Date

During each reporting period, the team members should report the actual date they began work on a task, the number of hours of actual work performed, and their estimate of the amount of remaining work hours on each task. When a task is completed, the team members will report the actual date that the work was completed.

To enter the Actual Start date, Actual Work, Remaining Work, and Actual Finish date in Microsoft Project 2003, complete the following steps:

1. Apply the Gantt Chart view
2. Right-click on the Select All button and select the Tracking table
3. "Best Fit" the Task Name column, if necessary
4. "Drag and drop" the Actual Work column between the Actual Start and Actual Finish columns
5. Right-click on the Actual Finish column header and click Insert Column from the shortcut menu
6. Select the Remaining Work column and click OK
7. Enter the actual start date of each resource assignment in the Actual Start column
8. Enter the actual work and remaining work estimates in their respective fields
9. When the task is completed, enter the completion date in the Actual Finish field

Figure 8-8 shows the Tracking table set up for entry of project progress using the Actual Work and Remaining Work method.

| | | Task Name | Act. Start | Act. Work | Remaining Work | Act. Finish | % Comp. | Phys. % Comp. | Act. Dur. | Rem. Dur. | Act. Cost |
|---|---|---|---|---|---|---|---|---|---|---|---|
| | 0 | ⊟ **Sample Project** | 3/14/05 | 40 h | 97 h | NA | 30% | 0% | 9.28 d | 21.21 d | $2,000.00 |
| | 1 | ⊟ **PHASE I** | 3/14/05 | 40 h | 97 h | NA | 32% | 0% | 9.3 d | 20.19 d | $2,000.00 |
| | 2 | Task A | 3/14/05 | 25 h | 0 h | 3/22/05 | 100% | 0% | 6.25 d | 0 d | $1,250.00 |
| | 3 | Task B | 3/24/05 | 15 h | 10 h | NA | 60% | 0% | 2.5 d | 1.67 d | $750.00 |
| | 4 | Task C | NA | 0 h | 40 h | NA | 0% | 0% | 0 d | 6.25 d | $0.00 |
| | 5 | Task D | NA | 0 h | 12 h | NA | 0% | 0% | 0 d | 4.55 d | $0.00 |
| | 6 | Task E | NA | 0 h | 35 h | NA | 0% | 0% | 0 d | 6.53 d | $0.00 |
| | 7 | Phase I Complete | NA | 0 h | 0 h | NA | 0% | 0% | 0 d | 1 d | $0.00 |

**Figure 8-8: Tracking table set up
for entry of Actual Work
and Remaining Work**

In Figure 8-8, the project manager scheduled 24 hours of Work on Task B. The team member performed 24 hours of Actual Work on the task; however, they have not completed the work. Therefore, the team member increased the Remaining Work estimate by 8 hours to show that they have not completed the work.

 When a team member adjusts the Remaining Work estimate, msProjectExperts recommends that you add a task Note to document the reason for changes in Remaining Work value. Doing so may assist in the estimating process in future projects.

151

# Hands On Exercise

## Exercise 8-3

Enter project progress using the Actual Work and Remaining Work method in the Project Master project.

1. Open the file called "Project Master08b" from your student folder

2. Apply the Tracking table and set it up for entry of actual progress using the Actual Work and Remaining Work method

3. Enter an Actual Start date of 01/02/07 for the task Order Server

4. Enter an Actual Finish date of 01/03/07 for the task Order Server

Notice that the Gantt bar for the task is marked as 100% Complete automatically. Notice also that the software calculates the Actual Work as 12 hours and sets the Remaining Work to 0 hours.

5. Enter an Actual Start date of 01/18/07 for the task Setup Server and Load O/S

Notice that the Gantt bar for this task moved two days later.

6. Enter a 8 hours of Actual Work for the task Setup Server and Load O/S, and adjust the Remaining Work value to 32 hours

Because the delivery of the new server was two days late, this task is two days behind schedule. Furthermore, because the resource increased the Remaining Work estimate, this means that the resource is even further behind schedule.

7. Insert a task note on the task Setup Server and Load O/S to document the reason for the task slippage

8. Save and close "Project Master08b"

### Daily Timesheet and Remaining Work

The most challenging method of tracking project progress requires your team members to enter their actual work hours in a daily timesheet. In addition, your team members must also give their estimate of the remaining work hours on each task at the end of the week.

This method of tracking progress is date-sensitive, since your team members will be able to show the actual start date of work on a task simply by entering their actual work hours in the timesheet for that day. They can also show an early finish for a task by entering actual work hours in the timesheet on the day the work was completed, and then adjusting the remaining work to 0 hours.

 msProjectExperts recommends that project team members record actual project progress on a daily basis, and submit their progress to the project manager on a weekly basis. Even though team members may protest, studies show that it takes an average of only 5 minutes per day to collect and record project progress.

# A "Best Practice" for Using the Timesheet

To enter actual progress using a timesheet, you should use the Resource Usage view, along with a four-step methodology recommended by msProjectExperts. The four steps for entering actual progress are as follows:

### Step #1 – Set up the Resource Usage View

The Resource Usage view consists of a Resource Sheet and the timephased grid (timesheet) as displayed in Figure 8-9. The Resource Usage view displays both resources and task assignments in the same view. In Figure 8-9, Ann Dyer is a resource and Tasks A is her task assignment in this particular project.

| | ⓘ | Resource Name | Work | Details | May 1, '05 S | M | T | W | T | F | S |
|---|---|---|---|---|---|---|---|---|---|---|---|
| | | ⊟ Unassigned | 0 h | Work | | | | | | | |
| | | *PHASE I COMPLETE* | *0 h* | Work | | | | | | | |
| 1 | | ⊟ Ann Dyer | 40 h | Work | | 8h | 8h | 8h | 8h | 8h | |
| | | *Task A* | *40 h* | Work | | 8h | 8h | 8h | 8h | 8h | |
| 2 | | ⊟ Brian Harry | 24 h | Work | | | | | | | |
| | | *Task B* | *24 h* | Work | | | | | | | |
| 3 | | ⊟ Kevin Holthaus | 64 h | Work | | 8h | 8h | 8h | 8h | 8h | |
| | | *Task A* | *40 h* | Work | | 8h | 8h | 8h | 8h | 8h | |
| | | *Task E* | *24 h* | Work | | | | | | | |
| 4 | | Mickey Cobb | 0 h | Work | | | | | | | |
| 5 | | ⊟ Mike Riley | 40 h | Work | | | | | | | |
| | | *Task D* | *40 h* | Work | | | | | | | |
| 6 | | Renee Hensley | 0 h | Work | | | | | | | |
| 7 | | ⊟ Sarah Baker | 56 h | Work | | | | | | | |
| | | *Task C* | *16 h* | Work | | | | | | | |
| | | *Task D* | *40 h* | Work | | | | | | | |
| | | | | Work | | | | | | | |

**Figure 8-9: Resource Usage view**

In the resource Table on the left side of the view, the software lists the resources in the same order as they are listed the Resource Sheet view. The software indents task assignments below each respective resource, and formats the assignments with italicized text. On the right side of the view, the timephased grid displays project data on a time sensitive basis (daily, weekly, monthly, etc.), such as Work hours, Baseline Work hours, and Actual Work hours.

Before you can enter actual progress in the Resource Usage view, you must set up the Resource Usage view by completing the following steps:

1. Click View ➤ Resource Usage

2. Zoom to Weeks over Days

3. Right-click anywhere in the timephased grid (yellow timesheet) and select Actual Work from the shortcut menu

4. Widen the Details column in the timephased grid, if necessary

5. Click Window ➤ Split to display the Resource Form in the lower pane

6. Right-click anywhere in the lower pane and select Work from the shortcut menu

7. Click the Resource Name column header to select all of the resources and their assignments in the column

8. Click the Hide Assignments button on the Formatting toolbar to roll up all of the task assignments

9. Expand the task assignments for the resource for whom you want to enter actual progress

Figure 8-10 shows the Resource Usage view, set up for entering Actual Work and Remaining Work values.

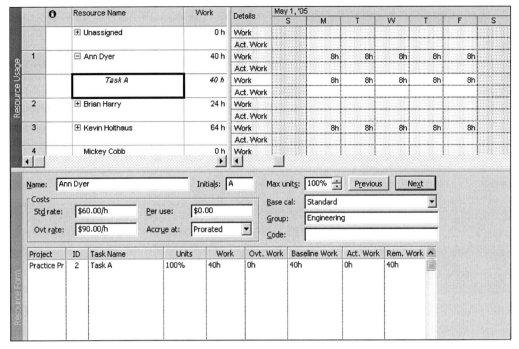

**Figure 8-10: Resource Usage view
set up to enter actual progress**

## Step #2 – Enter Actual Work

To enter actual work for a resource, complete the following steps:

1. Select the desired resource, then expand the resource's task assignments by clicking the minus sign (-) symbol in front of the resource's name

2. Select the Actual Work assignment cell in the timephased grid for the selected resource assignment

3. Type the actual work value in the Actual Work assignment cell

4. Press the right-arrow key, Tab key, or Enter key to enter the value in the cell

In Figure 8-11, I have entered actual progress for Ann Dyer on her Task A assignment during the week of May 1, 2005.

Figure 8-11: Actual Work entered
in timephased grid

In the timephased grid, the yellow cells are for the timephased values for the resources, and the white cells are the for the timephased values for task assignments. Be sure to enter your Actual Work hours in the white cells!

# Step #3 – Enter Zeroes When No Work Was Performed

There will probably be some days when team members perform no work on a task, although they have worked on the task on other days of the week. Rather than leaving the cell empty, the team members should a zero value (0) on days in which they performed no work. Doing so will cause the Remaining Work from a past time period to be rescheduled to the end of the task.

In Figure 8-12, Kevin Holthaus performed no work on Tuesday and Wednesday, and entered zero values for those two days. As a result, notice that the software has rescheduled the 16 hours of uncompleted work into the next work.

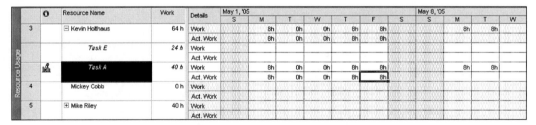

Figure 8-12: No work performed
on Tuesday and Wednesday

In Figure 8-12, Microsoft Project 2003 rescheduled the uncompleted work to the end of the task. For Fixed Duration tasks, however, the software evenly distributes the uncompleted work across the remaining task duration.

# Step #4 – Adjust Remaining Work Estimates

In addition to actual work hours, it is also a wise idea to ask resources to submit their Remaining Work estimate on in-progress tasks. For example, if a resource has performed 25 hours of actual work on a 40-hour task, their Remaining Work would be 15 hours. However, suppose the resource now believes that she cannot complete the task in the 15 hours scheduled, and should actually take 20 hours. The resource could then submit a new remaining work estimate of 20 hours to alert the project manager that her work has fallen behind schedule.

You will enter the Remaining Work estimate in the Remaining Work field in the Resource Form. To adjust the Remaining Work, complete the following sub-steps:

1. In the Resource Form (lower viewing pane), select the Remaining Work value for the correct resource assignment

2. Increase or decrease the Remaining Work value, as needed

3. Click the OK button in the Resource Form when finished

For example, Ann Dyer has completed 36 hours of Actual Work on the 40 hours of scheduled work on Task A. She does not believe she can complete the task in the remaining 4 hours of scheduled work, and has submitted a new Remaining Work estimate of 12 hours. Therefore, the project manager will adjust Ann Dyer's Remaining Work in the Resource Form, as displayed in Figure 8-13.

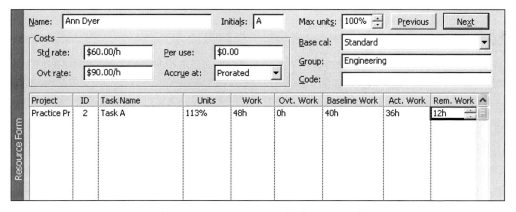

**Figure 8-13: Remaining Work
adjusted in Resource Form**

 It is also possible to adjust the Remaining Work value for a task assignment by double-clicking the task assignment for a resource, which will open the Assignment Information dialog. Click the Tracking tab, enter the Remaining Work for the selected Assignment, and click the OK button.

# Hands On Exercise

## Exercise 8-4

Use the "Best Practice" approach to enter task progress on a daily basis and to adjust the Remaining Work estimates in the Project Master project.

1. Open the file called "Project Master08c" from your student folder

2. Set up the Resource Usage view to follow the "Best Practice" for entering project progress in the timesheet

3. Enter actual progress for the following resources on a daily basis in the timephased grid and adjust the Remaining Work in the Resource Form

| Name: | Mickey Cobb | Week Of: | | | 12/31/06 | | |
|-------|-------------|----------|---|---|----------|---|---|
| Task Name | | M | T | W | Th | F | Rem. Work |
| Order Server | | | 8 | 2 | | | 0 |

| Name: | Jeff Holly | Week Of: | | | 01/14/07 | | |
|-------|------------|----------|---|---|----------|---|---|
| Task Name | | M | T | W | Th | F | Rem. Work |
| Setup Server and Load O/S | | | | | 4 | 4 | 32 |

4. Close the Resource Form (lower viewing pane)

5. Apply the Gantt Chart view

6. Zoom to Weeks Over Days

7. Select the task Order Server then click the Go To Selected Task button on the Standard toolbar

8. Save but *do not* close your "Project Master08c" project plan

## Exercise 8-5

The project manager received an e-mail message from Jeff Holly on the afternoon of 1/19/07. The text of the message read: "The server was delivered two days later than scheduled. Because of this delay, another project manager pulled me off this project to assist with her project, and I was only able to work half-time on setting up the server for our project." Add this project documentation in the form of a task Note.

1. Double-click the task, Setup Server and Load O/S

2. Select the Notes tab

3. Add the following bulleted Note to the task: "Server delivered two days late on 1/18/07. Resource borrowed half-time for another project."

4. Click the OK button when finished

5. Save but *do not* close your "Project Master08c" project plan

Your project should appear as shown in Figure 8-14.

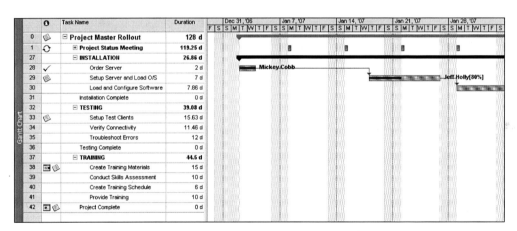

**Figure 8-14: Project Master after
actual progress entered on deliverables**

## Exercise 8-6

Enter project progress for the first two Project Status Meeting occurrences.

1. Apply the Task Usage view

2. Zoom to Months Over Weeks

3. Apply the Actual Work details to the timephased grid, and widen the Details column, if necessary

4. Select the task Project Status Meeting 1, then click the Go To Selected Task button to bring the Work hours into view

5. In the timephased grid, select the Actual Work summary cell (yellow cell) for the Project Status Meeting 1 task for the week of 1/7/07

6. Enter 10 hours of Actual Work for the week

Notice that software evenly distributed the 10 hours of Actual Work among the five resources assigned to this task.

7. In the timephased grid, enter 1 Ream of paper in the Actual Work cell for Status Meeting 1 for the week of 1/7/07

8. Roll up the Status Meeting 1 occurrence

9. Enter 10 hours of Actual Work and 1 Ream of paper for Status Meeting 2 for the week of 1/14/07

Your Task Usage view should appear as displayed in Figure 8-15.

| | 0 | Task Name | Work | Details | Jan '07 31 | 7 | 14 | 21 | 28 | Feb '07 4 |
|---|---|---|---|---|---|---|---|---|---|---|
| 0 | 📝 | ⊟ **Project Master Rollout** | **1,009 h** | Work | 10h | 10h | 18h | 42h | 38h | 32.85h |
| | | | | Act. Work | 10h | 10h | 18h | | | |
| 1 | 🔄 | ⊟ **Project Status Meeting** | **250 h** | Work | | 10h | 10h | 10h | 10h | 10h |
| | | | | Act. Work | | 10h | 10h | | | |
| 2 | ✓ | ⊞ Project Status Meeting 1 | 10 h | Work | | 10h | | | | |
| | | | | Act. Work | | 10h | | | | |
| 3 | ✓ | ⊟ Project Status Meeting 2 | 10 h | Work | | | 10h | | | |
| | | | | Act. Work | | | 10h | | | |
| | 📊 | Carolyn Fross | 2 h | Work | | | 2h | | | |
| | | | | Act. Work | | | 2h | | | |
| | 📊 | Helen Howard | 2 h | Work | | | 2h | | | |
| | | | | Act. Work | | | 2h | | | |
| | 📊 | Melena Keeth | 2 h | Work | | | 2h | | | |
| | | | | Act. Work | | | 2h | | | |
| | 📊 | Richard Sanders | 2 h | Work | | | 2h | | | |
| | | | | Act. Work | | | 2h | | | |
| | 📊 | Vicky Joslyn | 2 h | Work | | | 2h | | | |
| | | | | Act. Work | | | 2h | | | |
| | 📊 | Paper | 1 Reams | Work (Reams) | | | 1 | | | |
| | | | | Act. Work (Reams) | | | 1 | | | |

**Figure 8-15: Task Usage view
with Project Status Meeting progress**

10. Roll up the Status Meeting 2 occurrence

11. Apply the Gantt Chart view

12. Roll up the Project Status Meeting occurrences

13. Save and close your "Project Master08c" project plan

# Module 09

# Variance Analysis

## *Learning Objectives*

After completing this module, you will be able to:

- Understand project variance and the types of variance
- Understand the difference between "estimated" variance and "actual" variance
- Use a 4-step method to create custom Views using custom Tables, Filters, and Groups to meet your reporting needs
- Use the Organizer in Microsoft Project 2003

# Variance Defined

Variance analysis is the process of measuring actual progress and current estimates against the project baseline. Variance analysis provides the project manager with a means of identifying existing and/or potential problems, and is an important factor in revising the project plan to bring it back on track.

## *Types of Variance*

Since there are five task values that the software saves in a project baseline, there are also five types of task variance, which are:

- Duration variance

- Start variance

- Finish variance

- Work variance

- Cost variance

The most common types of variance which are of interest to you are work, cost, and date variance. It is important to identify all variance on a weekly basis; otherwise, the project can quickly slip out of your control.

The formula for calculating project variance is:

Variance = (Actuals + Remaining Estimates) - Baseline

What does variance mean? In Microsoft Project 2003, a positive variance is unfavorable to the project, while a negative variance is favorable to the project. For example, suppose that the Actual Work value for a task is 60 hours, the Remaining Work estimate is 40 hours, and the Baseline Work for the task is 80 hours. Using the above formula, we could calculate the work variance as:

Work Variance = (60 hours + 40 hours) – 80 hours

Work Variance = 100 hours - 80 hours

Work Variance = 20 hours

The resulting Work Variance of 20 hours is a positive variance that is unfavorable to the project because the Work hours are going over their original estimates. On the other hand, a negative variance is usually favorable to a project, indicating that a task is under budget on either work hours or cost, or has an early finish date.

## Actual and Estimated Variance

There are actually two general types of variance: actual variance and estimated variance. It is important that you understand the distinction between the two.

Actual variance occurs when an actual value, such as Actual Work, exceeds its baseline. For example, suppose that a task has a Baseline Work value of 40 hours, but the task is complete and the Actual Work on the task is 50 hours. Using the formula for Variance, we would calculate:

Work Variance = (50 hours + 0 hours) – 40 hours

Work Variance = 10 hours

Because the Actual Work exceeded the Baseline Work by 10 hours, we would describe this type of variance as Actual Variance. In other words, the task went over its budget on Work and it is too late for the project manager to do anything about it.

On the other hand, Estimated Variance is variance that "may" occur, based on the estimates submitted by the project team members. Estimated Variance occurs when actuals plus estimates (such as Actual Work + Remaining Work) exceeds the baseline. For example, suppose that a task has a Baseline Work value of 40 hours. At the end of the first week of work on the task, the resource reports 25 hours of Actual Work, plus a Remaining Work value (ETC) of 30 hours. Using the formula for Variance, we would calculate:

Work Variance = (25 hours + 30 hours) – 40 hours

Work Variance = 55 hours – 40 hours

Work Variance = 15 hours

The 15 hours of Work Variance is only an "estimate" at this point, which was caused by the resource working on the task to "estimate" that they have 15 hours more work to do than previously thought. Estimated Variance is very important to the project manager because it is variance that "might" occur while there is still time to adjust the project.

# Locating Variance in Microsoft Project 2003

The three most common types of variance that you will want to analyze are Work, Cost, and Date variance. To view each of these types of variance, apply the correct table in any task view, such as the Gantt Chart of Task Sheet view.

## *Work Variance*

You can view Work variance in the Work table, as shown in Figure 9-1. To apply the Work table, use either of the following methods:

- Click View ➤ Table ➤ Work

- Right-mouse click the Select All button, and then select Work

| | Task Name | Work | Baseline | Variance | Actual | Remaining | % W. Comp. |
|---|---|---|---|---|---|---|---|
| 0 | ⊟ **Sample Project** | **236 h** | **224 h** | **12 h** | **60 h** | **176 h** | **25%** |
| 1 | ⊟ **PHASE I** | **236 h** | **224 h** | **12 h** | **60 h** | **176 h** | **25%** |
| 2 | Task A | 92 h | 80 h | 12 h | 60 h | 32 h | 65% |
| 3 | Task B | 24 h | 24 h | 0 h | 0 h | 24 h | 0% |
| 4 | Task C | 16 h | 16 h | 0 h | 0 h | 16 h | 0% |
| 5 | Task D | 80 h | 80 h | 0 h | 0 h | 80 h | 0% |
| 6 | Task E | 24 h | 24 h | 0 h | 0 h | 24 h | 0% |
| 7 | PHASE I COMPLETE | 0 h | 0 h | 0 h | 0 h | 0 h | 0% |

**Figure 9-1: Gantt Chart view**
**Work table applied**

To analyze Work variance, examine each value in the Variance column. In Figure 9-1, the Project Summary Task (Row 0) reveals that this project is currently 12 hours over budget on work hours. Task A went 12 hours over budget and is not yet completed, thus, the Work variance on Task A is Estimated Variance (as opposed to Actual Variance).

 Microsoft Project 2003 calculates Work as the sum of Actual Work plus Remaining Work. It calculates Work Variance as the difference between the Work and Baseline Work.

## Cost Variance

You can view the cost variance for any project in the Cost table, as shown in Figure 9-2. To apply the Cost table, use either of the following methods:

- Click View ➢ Table ➢ Cost

- Right-mouse click the Select All button and then select Cost

| | Task Name | Fixed Cost | Fixed Cost Accrual | Total Cost | Baseline | Variance | Actual | Remaining |
|---|---|---|---|---|---|---|---|---|
| 0 | ⊟ **Sample Project** | **$0.00** | **Prorated** | **$14,160.00** | **$13,440.00** | **$720.00** | **$3,600.00** | **$10,560.00** |
| 1 | ⊟ **PHASE I** | **$0.00** | **Prorated** | **$14,160.00** | **$13,440.00** | **$720.00** | **$3,600.00** | **$10,560.00** |
| 2 | Task A | $0.00 | Prorated | $5,520.00 | $4,800.00 | $720.00 | $3,600.00 | $1,920.00 |
| 3 | Task B | $1,200.00 | Prorated | $2,400.00 | $2,400.00 | $0.00 | $0.00 | $2,400.00 |
| 4 | Task C | $0.00 | Prorated | $800.00 | $800.00 | $0.00 | $0.00 | $800.00 |
| 5 | Task D | $0.00 | Prorated | $4,000.00 | $4,000.00 | $0.00 | $0.00 | $4,000.00 |
| 6 | Task E | $0.00 | Prorated | $1,440.00 | $1,440.00 | $0.00 | $0.00 | $1,440.00 |
| 7 | PHASE I COMPLETE | $0.00 | Prorated | $0.00 | $0.00 | $0.00 | $0.00 | $0.00 |

**Figure 9-2: Gantt Chart view
Cost table applied**

To analyze Cost variance, examine each value in the Variance column. In Figure 9-2, the Project Summary Task (Row 0) reveals that the project is currently $720 over budget. This variance is because Task A is $720 over budget on cost.

## Date Variance

Date variance will be a major concern of every project manager, given that many projects have a firm finish date. To view the Date variance for any project, apply the Variance table as displayed in Figure 9-3. To apply the Variance table, use any of the following methods:

- Click View ➢ Table ➢ Variance

- Right-click the Select All button, and then select Variance

| | Task Name | Start | Finish | Baseline Start | Baseline Finish | Start Var. | Finish Var. |
|---|---|---|---|---|---|---|---|
| 0 | ⊟ **Sample Project** | **5/2/05** | **6/3/05** | **5/2/05** | **6/1/05** | **0 d** | **2 d** |
| 1 | ⊟ **PHASE I** | **5/2/05** | **6/3/05** | **5/2/05** | **6/1/05** | **0 d** | **2 d** |
| 2 | Task A | 5/2/05 | 5/10/05 | 5/2/05 | 5/6/05 | 0 d | 2 d |
| 3 | Task B | 5/11/05 | 5/16/05 | 5/9/05 | 5/12/05 | 2 d | 2 d |
| 4 | Task C | 5/17/05 | 5/19/05 | 5/13/05 | 5/17/05 | 2 d | 2 d |
| 5 | Task D | 5/19/05 | 5/26/05 | 5/17/05 | 5/24/05 | 2 d | 2 d |
| 6 | Task E | 5/26/05 | 6/3/05 | 5/24/05 | 6/1/05 | 2 d | 2 d |
| 7 | PHASE I COMPLETE | 6/3/05 | 6/3/05 | 6/1/05 | 6/1/05 | 2 d | 2 d |

**Figure 9-3: Gantt Chart view
Variance table applied**

To analyze Date variance, examine each value in the Start Variance and Finish Variance columns. In Figure 9-3, the Project Summary Task (Row 0) reveals that this project is 2 days late on its Finish date, caused by the late finish of Task A. Notice also that all of the other tasks are 2 days late as well. The project manager on this project will now want to determine whether to reschedule any of the tasks in the project to recapture some of the days lost by the late finish of Task A.

 msProjectExperts recommends that your company establish methodologies for the maximum amount of date slippage in a project before a project manager must take action.

# Using Views to Locate Variance

An experienced project manager once said, "Microsoft Project is like a black hole. It takes, but it won't give back." He was describing his frustration with gathering meaningful information about his projects. He knew the information was "in there somewhere" but he just could not find it! Using custom Views, you can quickly locate pertinent project information, including project variance.

## *What Is A View?*

End users of Microsoft Project 2003 define a View as a "way of looking at our data." In that regard, we are right. However, the software defines a View as follows:

View = Table + Filter + Group + Screen

In order to extract meaningful information from your projects, including Work, Cost, and Date Variance information, you must create your own custom Views so that you can see:

- The columns of data you want to see (the Table)

- Only the rows of data you want to see (the Filter)

- The organization of your desired data (the Group)

- Your data displayed on the screen using your desired layout (the Screen)

# Create a New View Using the 4-Step Method

You can create custom Views by following a 4-step method based on the definition of a View detailed previously. These four steps are:

1.  Select or create a Table

2.  Select or create a Filter

3.  Select or create a Group (most of the time this step is optional)

4.  Create a new View using the desired Table, Filter, Group, and Screen

## *Select or Create a Table*

The first step is to select an existing Table or to create a new Table if no existing Table meets your reporting needs. Remember, by definition, a Table is a collection of fields or columns. A key question to ask before attempting to create a View is, "What columns of data do I want to see in my new View?" The answer to this question will lead either to the selection of an existing Table, or to the creation of a new custom Table.

 A quick way to create a new Table is to copy an existing Table, and then to modify the copy. msProjectExperts reminds you that it is a "best practice" never to modify default Tables in Microsoft Project!

## *Select or Create a Filter*

The second step is to select an existing Filter, or to create a new Filter if no existing Filter meets your reporting needs. The Filter will extract the particular rows of data you wish to see. Before doing this step, it makes good sense to visually scan your project data first (known as applying an "eyeball filter") to determine exactly what data you want to extract from your project. Once you have either selected an existing Filter, or created a new Filter, it is also wise to test your Filter, to make sure the extracted data matches the anticipated results of your "eyeball filter."

## *Select or Create a Group*

The third step is to select an existing Group, or to create a new Group if no existing Group meets your reporting needs. In Microsoft Project 2003, Groups are a way of categorizing, sorting, and summarizing our extracted project data. Because very few default Groups exist in Microsoft Project 2003, it is very likely that you will need to create a new Group as a part of any new View.

## *Create the New Custom View*

The final step is to create a new custom View, which includes selecting a Screen. The Screen is a very important part of any custom View, as it controls how the software arranges the project data on the screen. Some of the common Screens from which we might choose are the Gantt Chart, Task Sheet, Task Usage, and Resource Usage screens. In Figure 9-4, I have selected the Gantt Chart option from the Screen drop-down list in the View Definition dialog.

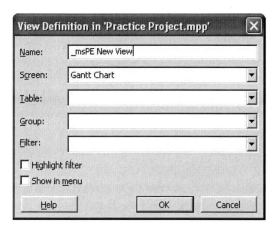

**Figure 9-4: View Definition
dialog**

In the View Definition dialog, the Screen choices are the same as many of the common Views that we can see in Microsoft Project 2003. When creating a new task View, our Screen choice will allow us to decide whether to include the Gantt Chart on the right of our new View (as with the Gantt Chart view), or whether the Task Sheet is displayed without a Gantt Chart (as with the Task Sheet view). Carefully study your Screen choices before completing the new View, as you cannot change the Screen when you edit the View!

# Hands On Exercise

## Exercise 9-1

You have been informed that the resource assigned to the task Create Training Materials has been pulled away from this project part of the time, and will only be able to devote 75% of each day to this task. Therefore, change the Units to 75% for the resource Ruth Andrews.

1. Open the file called "Project Master09" from your student folder

2. Apply the Task Entry view, and then select the task, Create Training Materials

3. Reduce the Units for Ruth Andrews to 75% and then click the OK button

4. If prompted by a Planning Wizard message, select the Continue option and then click the OK button

5. Close the lower viewing pane to return to the Gantt Chart view

Notice that the software has increased the Duration of this task to 20 days to compensate for the resource's reduced availability. Notice also that there is a Missed Deadline date indicator in the Indicators column for the task Provide Training. This means that the Finish date of the task has slipped past the internal Deadline date of 6/15/07.

6. Save but *do not* close your "Project Master09" project plan

## Exercise 9-2

As part of msPE's project management methodologies, tasks with 5 days or more date slippage warrant your immediate attention. Using the 4-step method, create a new View for reporting date variance greater than or equal to 5 days.

**Select or Create a Table:** Because the Variance table does not contain the columns you wish to see, create a new custom Variance table by completing the following steps.

1. Right-click on the Select All button and select More Tables

2. In the More Tables dialog, select the Variance table and click the Copy button

The software displays Table Definition dialog displays, as shown in Figure 9-5.

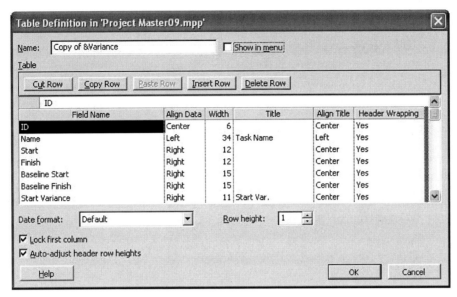

**Figure 9-5: Table Definition dialog**

3. Name the new table _msPE Date Variance and select the Show in menu option

4. Select the Name field in the Field Name column, then click the Insert Row button

5. Click the drop-down list for the blank row in the Field Name column, and select Indicators from the list of field names

6. For the Indicators field, set the Align Data value to Left, the Width value to 6, and the Align Title value to Left

7. Click the OK button, then click the Apply button

 msProjectExperts recommends that you use a unique naming convention when creating custom Views, Tables, Filters, or Groups. Your naming convention will separate your customization from the default Views, Tables, Filters, and Groups in Microsoft Project 2003. For example, this new Table was named "_msPE Date Variance" which would be easily distinguished from any of the default Tables.

8. Pull the vertical split bar all the way to the right side of the screen

**Rearrange the Table Columns:** You are not satisfied with the order of the columns in this custom Variance table. Therefore, use the "drag and drop" functionality of Microsoft Project 2003 to move the columns in the desired order.

1. Click and hold the column header of each of the columns that needs to be moved, and drag them into the following order:
   - ID
   - Indicators
   - Task Name
   - Finish Variance
   - Finish
   - Baseline Finish
   - Start Variance
   - Start
   - Baseline Start

When you rearrange the order of columns in any Table, Microsoft Project 2003 automatically changes the definition of that Table found in the Table Definition dialog.

2. Narrow the width of the Baseline Start and Baseline Finish columns to take advantage of the header text wrapping feature

3. Save but *do not* close your "Project Master09" file

**Select or Create a Filter:** Because there is no default Filter that extracts tasks whose Start Variance or Finish Variance is 5 days or greater, create a new Filter to accomplish this task by completing the following steps:

1. Examine the Finish Variance and Start Variance columns to "eyeball" for any tasks which have slipped 5 or more days

2. Click Project ➢Filtered for ➢ More Filters

3. Click the New button

The Filter Definition dialog displays, as shown in Figure 9-6.

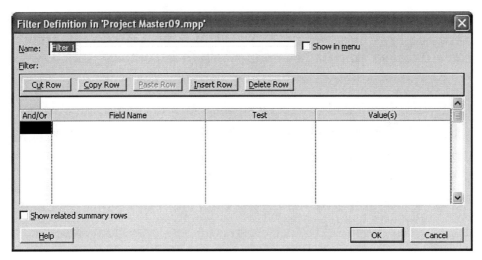

**Figure 9-6: Filter Definition dialog**

4. In the Filter Definition dialog, create a new Filter to match the specifications displayed in the following table:

| Name | _msPE Late Dates >= 5d | | |
|---|---|---|---|
| **Show in menu** | Selected | | |
| **And/Or** | **Field Name** | **Test** | **Value(s)s** |
| | Finish Variance | is greater than or equal to | 5d |
| Or | Start Variance | is greater than or equal to | 5d |
| **Show related summary rows** | Selected | | |

5. Click the OK button, then click the Apply button to test the new Filter against the results of your "eyeball filter"

6. Press the F3 key to apply the All Tasks filter

7. Reapply the Entry table and dock the vertical split bar on the right edge of the Duration column

8. Save but *do not* close your "Project Master09" project plan

**Select or Create a Group:** The project manager wants to group tasks based on Finish Variance in intervals of 5 days (0-5 days, 6-10 days, etc.). Because no default Group exists to accomplish this purpose, create a new Group by completing the following steps:

1. Click Project ➢Group by ➢ More Groups
2. Click the New button to open the Group Definition dialog
3. Name the new Group _msPE Finish Variance Interval 5d and select the Show in menu option
4. In the Group By field, select the Finish Variance field and set the Order to Descending

Figure 9-7 shows the completed Group Definition dialog.

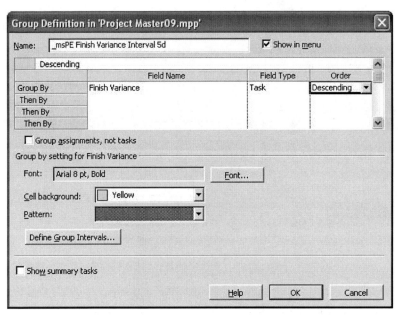

**Figure 9-7: Group Definition dialog**

In Microsoft Project 2003you can create a Group that will apply grouping on assignments in an Assignment view such as the Task Usage view. To do so, use the following additional options in the Group Definition dialog:

- Select the Group assignments, not tasks option
- Click the Field Type drop-down list for the field and select Assignments

5. Click Define Group Intervals button

6. In the Define Group Interval dialog, select Days in the Group on: field, and then select 5 in the Group interval field

The Define Group Interval dialog is displayed in Figure 9-8.

**Figure 9-8: Define Group Interval dialog**

7. Click OK to close the Define Group Interval dialog, and then click OK to close the Group Definition dialog

8. Click the Close button in the More Groups dialog (do not apply this new Group yet)

**Create a New View:** Create a new View to show date variance of greater than or equal to 5 days. Use your new custom Table, Filter, and Group in this new custom View.

1. Click View ➢ More Views

The More Views dialog opens, as displayed in Figure 9-9.

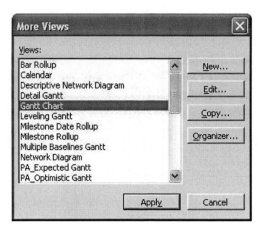

**Figure 9-9: More Views
dialog**

2.  In the More Views dialog, click the New button

The Define New View dialog opens, as shown in Figure 9-10.

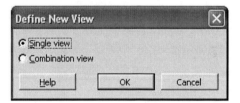

**Figure 9-10: Define New
View dialog**

3.  Select the Single view option then click OK

The View Definition dialog opens, as shown in Figure 9-11.

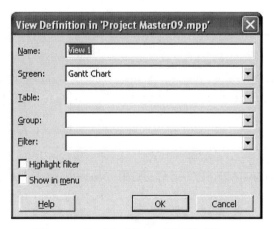

**Figure 9-11: View Definition
dialog**

4. In the View Definition dialog, enter the information contained in the following table:

| Name | _msPE Late Dates >= 5d |
|---|---|
| **Screen** | Task Sheet |
| **Table** | _msPE Date Variance |
| **Group** | _msPE Finish Variance Interval 5d |
| **Filter** | _msPE Late Dates >= 5d |
| **Show in menu** | Selected |

When creating a new View, you must select a Group, even if you do not want to use a Group in your View. If you fail to select a Group, you will receive an error message when you click the OK button.

If the Highlight Filter option is selected, a View will display all tasks, but will highlight in blue only those tasks that meet the Filter criteria.

5. Click the OK button and then click the Apply button

Your project should appear as is displayed in Figure 9-12.

| | | ⓘ | Task Name | Finish Var. | Finish | Baseline Finish | Start Var. | Start | Baseline Start |
|---|---|---|---|---|---|---|---|---|---|
| | | | ⊟ **Finish Variance: 10 d - <15 d** | **0 d** | **6/18/07** | **5/31/07** | **0 d** | **4/9/07** | **3/28/07** |
| | 38 | | Create Training Materials | 12.39 d | 5/7/07 | 4/18/07 | 7.39 d | 4/9/07 | 3/28/07 |
| | 39 | | Conduct Skills Assessment | 11.89 d | 5/17/07 | 5/1/07 | 11.89 d | 5/3/07 | 4/17/07 |
| | 40 | | Create Training Schedule | 11.89 d | 5/25/07 | 5/9/07 | 11.89 d | 5/17/07 | 5/1/07 |
| | 41 | | Provide Training | 11.89 d | 6/18/07 | 5/31/07 | 11.89 d | 6/4/07 | 5/16/07 |
| | | | ⊟ **Finish Variance: 5 d - <10 d** | **0 d** | **4/9/07** | **3/28/07** | **0 d** | **1/29/07** | **1/23/07** |
| | 30 | | Load and Configure Software | 7.39 d | 2/13/07 | 2/1/07 | 4 d | 1/29/07 | 1/23/07 |
| | 31 | | Installation Complete | 7.39 d | 2/13/07 | 2/1/07 | 7.39 d | 2/13/07 | 2/1/07 |
| | 33 | | Setup Test Clients | 7.39 d | 3/6/07 | 2/23/07 | 7.39 d | 2/13/07 | 2/1/07 |
| | 34 | | Verify Connectivity | 7.39 d | 3/22/07 | 3/12/07 | 7.39 d | 3/6/07 | 2/23/07 |
| | 35 | | Troubleshoot Errors | 7.39 d | 4/9/07 | 3/28/07 | 7.39 d | 3/22/07 | 3/12/07 |
| | 36 | | Testing Complete | 7.39 d | 4/9/07 | 3/28/07 | 7.39 d | 4/9/07 | 3/28/07 |

**Figure 9-12: _msPE Late Dates > 5d
view applied**

6. Reapply the Gantt Chart view

7. Save but *do not* close your "Project Master09" project plan

## Exercise 9-3

Create a new custom Tracking Gantt view using the new custom Table and Filter created in Exercise 9-2. When creating the new View, apply the custom filter as a Highlight filter.

1. Click View ➢ More Views

2. Select the Tracking Gantt view and click the Copy button

3. In the View Definition dialog, enter the information contained in the following table:

| Name | _msPE Tracking Gantt |
|---|---|
| Table | _msPE Date Variance |
| Group | No Group |
| Filter | _msPE Late Dates >= 5d |
| Highlight filter | Selected |
| Show in menu | Selected |

4. Click the OK button and then click the Apply button

5. Click the Close button

Your project should appear as is displayed in Figure 9-13.

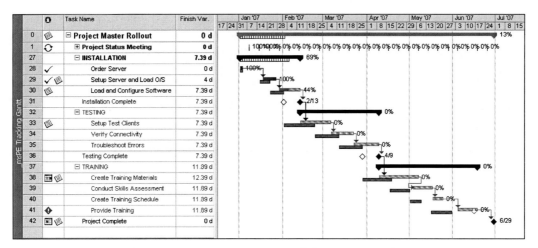

**Figure 9-13: _msPE Tracking Gantt view**

6. Reapply the Gantt Chart view

7. Save but do not close your "Project Master09" project plan

# Using the Organizer

When you create a custom View, along with a custom Table, a custom Filter, and a custom Group, those four custom objects exist only in the active project. In Microsoft Project 2003, you can use the Organizer to manage any of the custom objects that are created in a project plan. These objects can include any of the following:

- Views
- Tables
- Forms
- Filters
- Groups
- Reports
- Fields
- Calendars
- Toolbars
- Maps
- Modules

To access the Organizer, click Tools ➢ Organizer. The software opens the Organizer dialog as shown in Figure 9-14.

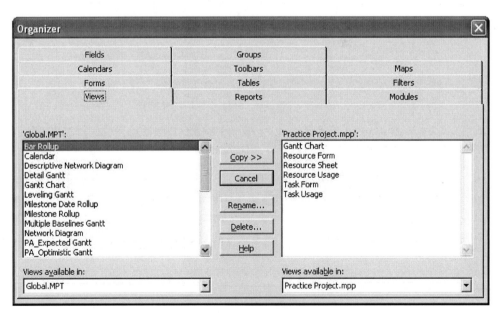

**Figure 9-14: Organizer
dialog**

When you create a new custom object in a project plan, you can use the Organizer to manage this new object by doing any of the following:

- Copying the custom object to the Global.mpt file
- Copying the custom object to another project file
- Renaming the custom object
- Deleting the custom object

 The Global.mpt file is the master template used for creating all new blank project files. The Global.mpt file can be understood as each user's personal library of custom objects, such as custom Views, Tables, Filters, Groups, etc. In order to make a custom object accessible to all present and future project plans, the user must copy these custom objects to the Global.mpt file.

To copy a custom object to the Global.mpt file, complete the following steps:

1. Select proper tab for the type of object (such as a Filter or a View)
2. Select the object(s) to be copied from the Available in list on the right side of the Organizer dialog
3. Click the Copy button in the middle of the dialog

To delete a custom object that is no longer needed, select the name of the object and then click the Delete button. To rename an object, select the name of the object and then click the Rename button. To copy custom objects from one project file to another, do the following:

1. Open both project files
2. Click the Views Available In drop-down list on the *left side* of the dialog, and select the name of the *first* project file
3. Click the Views Available In drop-down list on the *right side* of the dialog, and select the name of the *second* project file
4. Select the tab for the type of object
5. Select the custom object on either side of the dialog and click the Copy button

# Hands On Exercise

## Exercise 9-4

Copy the new custom Views, Tables, Filters, and Groups created in Exercises 9-2 and 9-3 from the project file to your Global.mpt file by using the Organizer.

1. Click Tools ≻Organizer

2. Using the Control key, select the _msPE Late Dates >= 5d and _msPE Tracking Gantt views on the right side of the dialog (contained in the Project Master09.mpp file)

3. Click the Copy button to copy these Views to the left side of the dialog (to the Global.mpt file)

4. Click the Tables tab and copy the _msPE Date Variance table to the Global.mpt

5. Click the Filters tab and copy the _msPE Late Dates >= 5d filter to the Global.mpt

6. Click the Groups tab and copy the __msPE Finish Variance Interval 5d group to the Global.mpt

7. Click the Close button when finished

 When you are using the Organizer to copy a new custom View to the Global.mpt, don't forget to copy any new Tables, Filters, or Groups you may have created in the process. Otherwise your new View will not work in other projects.

 The custom View, Tables, and Filter were copied only to the copy of the Global.mpt file. When you exit out of Microsoft Project 2003, these changes to the Global.mpt file will then be saved to your hard drive.

# Module 10

## Plan Revision

### Learning Objectives

After completing this module, you will be able to:

- Define plan revision
- Understand how to revise a plan
- Understand and use the Tracking Gantt view
- Revise a project plan in Microsoft Project 2003

# Plan Revision Defined

Once you have completed variance analysis, it may be necessary to revise your project plan. If your project is beginning to deviate from its original plan, it is important to realign your plan with its initial objectives and bring the project "back on track."

There are a number of strategies for revising the project plan, but each requires careful analysis prior to implementation. You would be wise to perform a "what-if" analysis before making plan revisions, especially if you need formal approval to make plan revisions.

As part of your organization's project management methodologies, you should define strategies for plan revision for tasks, deliverables, phases, and the overall project. Project documentation revisions may be necessary as well.

## *Methods for Plan Revision*

Microsoft Project 2003 offers a number of methods for revising a project plan. These methods include the following:

- Modify mandatory dependencies to shorten the duration of dependent tasks

- Reduce or remove Lag time to shorten the calendar time of dependent tasks

- Increase the working time for a resource

- Add overtime

- Add resources to effort-driven tasks

- Reduce the scope (feature set) of the project

- Problems with Plan Revision

Prior to implementing one or more of the above techniques, you must be aware of potential problems that may arise because of implementing these techniques. Some of the potential problems include:

- Reducing built-in lag time for risk creates a riskier environment for the project. "Gambling with risk may cause more harm than good."

- Adding resources to effort-driven tasks may actually increase the total effort (work) due to increased communication needs.

- Adding overtime on a regular basis may lead to a higher employee turnover rate.

- The project scope may be non-negotiable.

Whatever the case may be, you must perform a careful analysis in realigning the project with the project's strategic objectives.

 Plan Revision is usually a consequence of Variance Analysis, which you will do because of project variance that is moving the project away from its original goals. Remember that revising a plan will cause additional project variance, which you must also analyze, and which could perhaps lead to additional plan revision! For example, using overtime work to shorten the Duration of a task will cause increased cost variance.

## Using the Tracking Gantt View

You will find that the Tracking Gantt view is especially useful during plan revision, as it visually compares the current state of the project against the original project plan (the project baseline). To access the Tracking Gantt view, click View ➢ Tracking Gantt. Figure 10-1 shows the Tracking Gantt view.

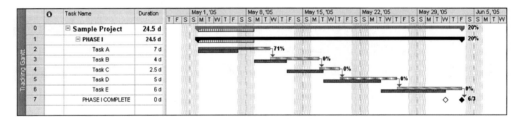

**Figure 10-1: Tracking Gantt View**

To understand the Tracking Gantt view requires some explanation. Following is a description of the major components of the Tracking Gantt view:

- Light blue Gantt bars represent planned work not on the Critical Path

- Dark blue Gantt bars represent completed work not on the Critical Path

- Light red Gantt bars represent tasks on the Critical Path

- Dark red Gantt bars represent completed work on a Critical Task

- Gray Gantt bars represent the Baseline for each task

- The percentage value at the right end of each Gantt bar is the % Complete field (% of Duration complete), not % Work Complete

- The "fence post" pattern on each summary task Gantt bar is the cumulative % Complete for all of its sub-tasks

186

The Critical Path in any project plan consists of "those tasks which cannot slip without impacting the finish date of the project." Tasks on the Critical Path are Critical Tasks.

Using the Tracking Gantt view allows to see slippage in a project. In Figure 10-1, it is easy to see that Task A is 2 days late, which is causing the slippage of all successor tasks and ultimately the finish date of the entire project. At this point, you can determine whether you can revise any successor tasks to bring the project back on its original schedule.

# Hands On Exercise

## Exercise 10-1

Analyze project slippage in the Project Master project.

1. Open the file called "Project Master10" from your student folder

2. Click View ➤ Tracking Gantt

3. Click the Go To Selected Task button on the Standard toolbar to bring the Gantt bars into view

4. Zoom to Months Over Weeks

Notice the following aspects of the Project Master Rollout project:

- The task Setup Server and Load O/S started late, which then led to a late finish.

- The task Load and Configure Software started late, and because the Remaining Work estimate was increased, it will finish even later.

- Because of the Finish date slippage of the task, Setup Server and Load O/S and Load and Configure Software, all successor tasks in the project will start and finish late as well.

- Because of the resource availability issue on the task, Create Training Materials, this task will finish late, which will cause all of the tasks in the TRAINING phase to start and finish late as well.

## Exercise 10-2

Revise the Project Master plan to bring the project back on track against baseline schedule.

1. Select the task Load and Configure Software

2. Click the Window menu, then click Split

3. In the Task Form, add Renee Hensley at 30% Units (do not enter a Work value) and click the OK button

**Student Challenge**: If our intent was the shorten the Duration of this task using effort-driven scheduling, why didn't we add Renee Hensley at 70% Units or even 100% Units?

By using effort-driven schedule, we have saved approximately 2 days against its previous Finish date.

Dave Harbaugh is able to work only 40% of each day on the task, Setup Test Clients, due to commitments to another project. You have "negotiated" with the other project manager to "borrow" Dave Harbaugh for a little extra time on this task to complete it sooner.

4. Select the task Setup Test Clients and increase the Units for Dave Harbaugh to 50%

Notice that this action saved 3 days and allows for an earlier Start for all of the subtasks in both the TESTING and TRAINING summary tasks. You have determined, however, that you must address the severe slippage on the task Create Training Materials.

5. Select the task Create Training Materials

6. Using effort-driven scheduling, add Kent Bergstrand at 50% Units (do not enter a Work value) and click the OK button

 **Student Challenge:** If our intent was to shorten the Duration of this task using effort-driven scheduling, why didn't we simply add Kent Bergstrand at 100% Units to this task?

Due to increased communication needs between the resources assigned to this task, increase the Work for Ruth Andrews to 80 hours and increase the Work for Kent Bergstrand to 56 hours

 **Reminder:** MsProjectExperts recommends that when adding resources to a task using effort-driven scheduling, and the resources are going to work together, you should increase the Work hours for each resource in the range of 10% to 20% to account for their increased communications needs.

7.  Close the Task form to return to a single-pane Tracking Gantt view

In order to "fast track" the schedule in the TRAINING phase, you have made a decision to begin the skill assessments after the training developer has finished approximately 75% of the training materials.

8.  Set a -25% Lag on the FS dependency between the tasks Create Training Materials and Conduct Skills Assessment

In Figure 10-2, notice that now the project is back on schedule compared to its original baseline schedule.

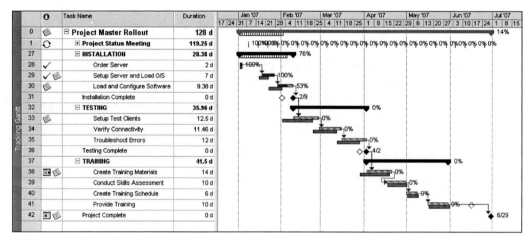

**Figure 10-2: Project Master
after plan revisions**

9.  Save and close your "Project Master10" project plan

# Module 11

# Change Control

## *Learning Objectives*

After completing this module, you will be able to:

- Define change control

- Understand Baseline issues relating to change control

- Understand how Autolink automatically sets task dependencies when inserting new tasks in a project with dependencies

- Use change control procedures to add a new task to a project in Microsoft Project 2003 and to baseline the new task

# Change Control Defined

According to the Project Management Institute, "Integrated Change Control is concerned with (a) influencing the factors that create changes to ensure that changes are agreed upon, (b) determining that a change has occurred, and (c) managing the actual changes when and as they occur." – PMBOK, 2000

Effective change control management identifies and maximizes the benefits of change, and manages change as it occurs. You should document the process of change control management in the Statement of Work, along with the "rules of engagement" regarding change. Both the project sponsor and other interested parties should "sign off" on the change control procedures and rules of engagement as needed. Once enacted, even these change control procedures should be subject to the change control process!

# Baseline Issues with Change Control

The need for project Change Control procedures also drives the need for procedures to baseline a project after new tasks have been added via Change Control. You should not rebaseline your project by saving the baseline in the original Baseline field. Instead, there are additional ways in Microsoft Project 2003 to rebaseline a project. These methods include:

- Save the new baseline to one of the ten additional Baseline fields, Baseline1 through Baseline 10
- Save the baseline for only the selected tasks, and "roll up" the new baseline values to the appropriate summary tasks

### *Save Baseline for Selected Tasks*

In earlier versions of Microsoft Project, saving a baseline for selected tasks created a challenging situation. Because the baseline information for subtasks did not roll up to their respective summary tasks, this created a tremendous amount of project variance, with a proportionate amount of headaches for the project manager!

In Microsoft Project 2003, when it is necessary to baseline only selected tasks, it is your choice whether to roll up the baseline values for subtasks to their respective summary tasks. To save a baseline only for selected tasks, complete the following steps:

1. Select the tasks to be baselined
2. Click Tools ➤ Tracking ➤ Save Baseline
3. Select the Save Baseline option and select Baseline from the drop-down list of baseline fields
4. In the For: section, select Selected tasks

5. In the Roll up baselines: section, select either To all summary tasks or From subtasks into selected summary tasks, if you want the baseline information rolled up to one or more summary tasks

6. Click the OK button

Figure 11-1 shows the Save Baseline dialog with settings for saving a baseline for selected tasks only.

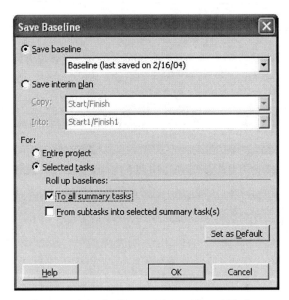

**Figure 11-1: Save Baseline Dialog**
**Baseline Only Selected Tasks**

 Using the preceding procedure will not destroy the data in your original Baseline field. Rather, it will "adjust" the original project baseline by adding the baseline data from the newly added tasks. In a sense, this procedure will treat the new tasks as if they were part of the project at the very beginning, and will eliminate any project variance caused by adding new tasks to the project.

## *Inserting New Tasks between Dependent Tasks*

When you insert new tasks into a project in which you have already set task dependencies, you should be aware of the "Autolink" feature of Microsoft Project 2003. When you insert new tasks between two dependent tasks, Microsoft Project 2003 will attempt to link the new tasks automatically with the dependent tasks.

If the dependent tasks have a Finish-to-Start (FS) dependency, the software will automatically link the new tasks with the existing tasks using an FS dependency. On the other hand, if you insert new tasks between two tasks which have any other type of dependency (SS, FF, or SF), then Microsoft Project 2003 will not automatically link the new tasks.

 Because you should always make task dependency decisions, msProjectExperts recommends that you break the task dependency links between tasks in the section where you will insert the new tasks. Once you have inserted the new tasks, and then establish appropriate task dependencies for tasks in that section of your project plan.

 The Autolink feature of Microsoft Project 2003 is set on the Schedule page of the project Options dialog. The default setting for the Autolink inserted or moved tasks is checked. msProjectExperts recommends that you do not change this option, otherwise you will see unexpected behavior when moving linked tasks.

# Hands On Exercise

## Exercise 11-1

The project sponsor is concerned that some of the users of the Project Master software may not have the knowledge of project management theory that they need to use the software effectively. Therefore, the project sponsor has requested that you add an additional task, Provide PM Theory Training, to the project.

The project sponsor completed Change Request Form #CRF100-01 and the Project Management Office audited the form. The project team completed an impact analysis at a total cost of $500 to the project sponsor. The Change Control Board granted approval for the change. Add this new task to the Project Master project.

1. Open the file called "Project Master11" from your student folder

2. Select the two tasks, Create Training Schedule and Provide Training, then click the Unlink Tasks button on the Standard toolbar

3. Select the task Provide Training, then press the Insert key on the keyboard to insert a blank task before the Provide Training task

4. In the blank line, insert a new task named Provide PM Theory Training and leave the Duration at the default of 1 day

5. Create the following predecessor/successor dependencies:

   - **FS + 5 Lag:** Create Training Schedule and Provide PM Theory Training

   - **SS + 2d Lag:** Provide PM Theory Training and Provide Training

6. Assign Marilyn Ray to the task Provide PM Theory Training at 100% units and 56 hours of work

7. Add a note to the task Provide PM Theory Training, indicating that it was added to the plan as a result of CRF100-01 and at a cost to the project sponsor of $500

8. Apply the Cost table and enter a Fixed Cost of $500 to the task Provide PM Theory Training

Your project should appear as is displayed in Figure 11-2.

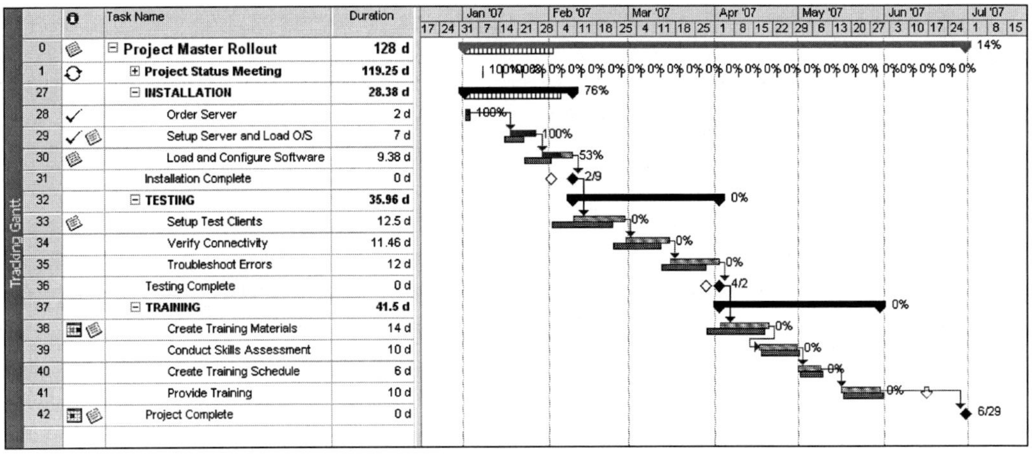

**Figure 11-2: Project Master after
CRF100-01 Change Control procedure**

9. Save but do not close your "Project Master11" file

# Exercise 11-2

The company methodology for baselining tasks added via Change Control procedures is to baseline only the new tasks, and to roll up the baseline values to all summary tasks which are impacted by the new tasks. Therefore, save a baseline the new task using the company's baselining methodology.

1. Apply the Baseline table, then drag the vertical split bar all the way to the right side of the screen

Notice the current values for the Baseline Work and Baseline Cost fields for the Project Summary Task (Row 0) and for the TRAINING summary task. Notice also that there is no Baseline information saved for the new task, Provide PM Theory Training.

2. Select the new task, Provide PM Theory Training

3. Click Tools ➢ Tracking ➢ Save Baseline

4. Make sure the Save Baseline option is selected, along with the Baseline field

5. In the For: section, select Selected tasks

6. In the Roll up baselines: section, select To all summary tasks, and click the OK button when finished

7. When warned about overwriting the data in the baseline, click the OK button in the Microsoft Project warning dialog

Notice that the Baseline Work and Baseline Cost values for the Project Summary Task (Row 0) and the TRAINING summary task have each been "adjusted" to include the 56 hours of Baseline Work and the $2,240 of Baseline Cost from the new task, Provide PM Theory Training. Notice also that the software has preserved the remainder of the Baseline data for the project.

 If you re-examine the Work and Cost tables, you will find that the variance in these tables is from Work and Cost going over budget, and by the plan revision performed to bring the project back on schedule. The change control procedure is not the cause of any of the Work and Cost variance, which will make it easier to interpret our project variance to the project sponsor.

8. Reapply the Entry table and pull the vertical split bar back to the right edge of the Duration column

9. Save and close your "Project Master11" project plan

# Module 12

## Printing and Reporting

### Learning Objectives

After completing this module, you will be able to:

- Understand project communications management
- Understand the importance of identifying Stakeholder reporting needs
- Print project Views and Reports, and create custom Reports in Microsoft Project 2003

# Project Communications Management

Project communications management provides the communication links between the project team and all groups interested in the project. All project participants must communicate at some level throughout the project life cycle; therefore, you should possess a thorough understanding of your organization's communications methodologies and project reporting mechanisms.

### *Identifying Stakeholder Reporting Needs*

Prior to executing the project, you should meet with key project stakeholders to determine their reporting needs. You should gather the following information:

- What project information needs to be reported

- How the project reports need to be presented

- How often project information needs to be reported

Once you have gathered this information, you should create any new Views, Tables, Filters, Groups, and Reports in Microsoft Project 2003 to meet these reporting needs.

# Reporting in Microsoft Project 2003

Microsoft Project 2003 contains six categories of pre-formatted Reports. To select and print a Report, complete the following steps:

1. Click View ➢ Reports

The software opens the Reports dialog as shown in Figure 12-1.

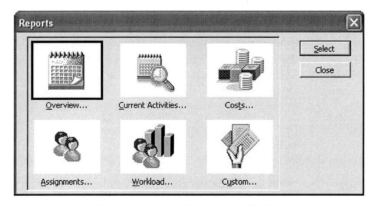

**Figure 12-1: Reports dialog**

2. Select a category, such as the Overview category, and then and click the Select button

The software displays the Overview Reports dialog, as shown in Figure 12-2.

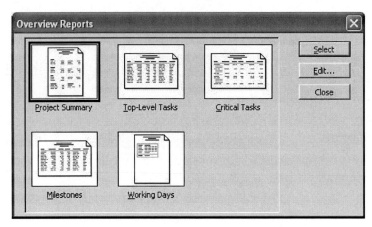

**Figure 12-2: Overview Reports dialog**

3. Select one of the Overview reports, such as the Project Summary report

The software displays a print preview the report, as shown in Figure 12-3.

**Sample Project**
**msProjectExperts**
**Gary Chefetz**
as of 2/17/04

Dates

| | | | |
|---|---|---|---|
| Start: | 5/2/05 | Finish: | 6/3/05 |
| Baseline Start: | 5/2/05 | Baseline Finish: | 6/1/05 |
| Actual Start: | 5/2/05 | Actual Finish: | NA |
| Start Variance: | 0 d | Finish Variance: | 2 d |

Duration

| | | | |
|---|---|---|---|
| Scheduled: | 24.5 d | Remaining: | 19.5 d |
| Baseline: | 22.5 d | Actual: | 5 d |
| Variance: | 2 d | Percent Complete: | 20 % |

Work

| | | | |
|---|---|---|---|
| Scheduled: | 236 h | Remaining: | 176 h |
| Baseline: | 224 h | Actual: | 60 h |
| Variance: | 12 h | Percent Complete: | 25 % |

Costs

| | | | |
|---|---|---|---|
| Scheduled: | $14,160.00 | Remaining: | $10,560.00 |
| Baseline: | $13,440.00 | Actual: | $3,600.00 |
| Variance: | $720.00 | | |

| Task Status | | Resource Status | |
|---|---|---|---|
| Tasks not yet started: | 5 | Work Resources: | 7 |
| Tasks in progress: | 2 | Overallocated Work Resources: | 0 |
| Tasks completed: | 0 | Material Resources: | 0 |
| Total Tasks: | 7 | Total Resources: | 7 |

Notes

Use this project to display sample screens in Microsoft Project 2003.

**Figure 12-3: Print Preview:**
**Project Summary Report**

4. Click the Print button at the top of the Print Preview dialog to go to the Print dialog

5. In the Print dialog, make any printing selections you wish, then click the OK button to print the report

Following is a description of the five categories of default Reports:

| Overview Reports | |
|---|---|
| Project Summary | An overview of Dates, Duration, Work, Costs, Tasks, and Resources |
| Top-Level Tasks | Displays tasks at the highest outline level |
| Critical Tasks | Displays critical tasks |
| Milestones | Displays project milestones |
| Working Days | Displays working days and exceptions |

| Current Activities Reports | |
|---|---|
| Unstarted Tasks | Displays tasks that have not started |
| Tasks Starting Soon | Displays tasks starting in a user-defined time period |
| Task in Progress | Displays tasks that have started but have not yet finished |
| Completed Tasks | Displays tasks where both the %Complete and %Work Complete fields are set to 100% |
| Should Have Started Tasks | Displays tasks that should start by a user-defined time period |
| Slipping Tasks | Displays tasks where the current estimated finish date is later than the baseline finish date |

| Cost Reports | |
|---|---|
| Cash Flow | Displays costs timephased in one-week time periods |
| Budget | Displays the budget for all tasks, sorted from the highest cost to the lowest cost |
| Overbudget Tasks | Displays tasks where the current estimated cost is greater than the baseline cost |
| Overbudget Resources | Displays resources where the current estimated cost is greater than the baseline cost |
| Earned Value | Displays earned value information |

| Assignment Reports | |
|---|---|
| Who Does What | Displays usage information for all resources |
| Who Does What When | Displays resource work timephased over one-day time periods |
| To-do List | Displays tasks for a user-defined resource |
| Overallocated Resources | Displays resources that are overallocated |

| Workload Reports | |
|---|---|
| Task Usage | Displays task usage information timephased over one-week time periods |
| Resource Usage | Displays resource usage information timephased over one-week time periods |

## Reports Based on Views

When printing Reports in Microsoft Project 2003, remember that the software bases Reports on Views (namely, a Table and a Filter). When a View and Report share the same Table and Filter, what is currently visible in the View will be visible in the Report, and what is not currently visible in the View will not be visible in the Report.

Keep the following points in mind when printing any of the default Reports in Microsoft Project 2003:

- Most task Reports use the task list that is visible in the Task Sheet. Tasks that are rolled up in their respective summary tasks in the Task Sheet will not be visible in most task Reports. This is true of all six Reports in the Current Activities section.

- Most resource Reports use the resource list that is visible in the Resource Sheet. The Overbudget Resources and Overallocated Resources reports use the resource list found in the Resource Sheet view.

- The software bases the Cash Flow report on the Task Usage view. Tasks that are rolled up in their respective summary task in the Task Usage view will not be visible in the Cash Flow report.

- The software bases the Who Does What When report on the Resource Usage view. Any task assignments that are rolled up to their respective resource in the Resource Usage view will not be visible in the Who Does What When report.

- Obviously, the software bases the Task Usage and Resource Usage reports on the Task Usage and Resource Usage views.

# Creating Custom Reports

What is a Report? To the user of the Microsoft Project 2003, a Report seems to be project information printed on paper. In that regard, we are not wrong. However, from the perspective of the software, a Report can be generally defined as:

**Report = Table + Filter + Report Details**

The definition of a Report is very similar to the definition of a View. In fact, because Reports and Views are closely related, you can use a 3-step method to create a Report in much the same way as you use the 4-step method to create a View. These three steps are as follows:

1. Select or create a Table

2. Select or create a Filter

3. Create the new Report, using your Table and Filter, with your desired Details and Sorting

Many times, we will create a Report using the same Tables and Filters that we used to create a View. In such cases, it is easiest to create our Report immediately after creating the View, as the Table and Filter used in the View will be fresh in our memory.

To create a custom report, double-click the Custom Reports icon in the Reports dialog. The software displays the Custom Reports dialog, as shown in Figure 12-4.

**Figure 12-4: Custom Reports dialog**

To understand how to create a custom Report, it is helpful to view the definition of existing Reports. Once you understand how the definitions of default Reports, you can easily copy a default Report and modify the copy to meet your reporting needs.

In the Custom Reports dialog, you can view the definition of a Report by selecting the report and clicking the Edit button. For example, Figure 12-5 shows the definition of the Unstarted Tasks report.

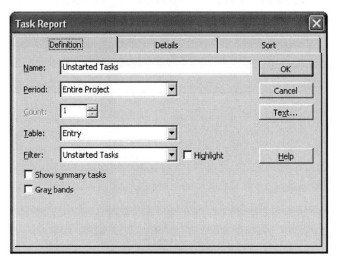

**Figure 12-5: Unstarted Tasks Report
dialog, Definition page**

The Unstarted Tasks Report consists of the Entry table and the Unstarted Tasks filter. On the Definition page of this dialog, you can also see other details for the Report, such the Highlight filter option, the time Period drop-down list, and the options to Show summary tasks and Gray bands on the report. Gray bands are used to separate sections of data in a report.

 When you select the Highlight option in the definition of a task Report, all tasks will be printed in your Report. However, those tasks that meet your filter criteria will be "highlighted" with a gray bar. You should experiment with this option before using it.

Additional definition information for this Report can be found by clicking the Details tab in this dialog. Figure 12-6 shows the Details page, where you can see these other additional details which may be printed, such as Task and Assignment information, Borders, Gridlines, and Totals for the values in a Report.

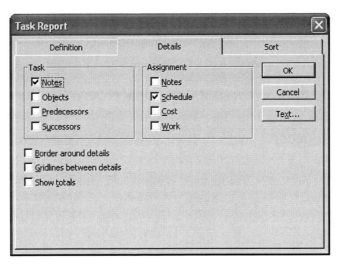

**Figure 12-6: Unstarted Tasks Report
dialog, Details Page**

 The Notes option is a useful detail to add to any custom Report definition. In reports you use to display project variance, adding the Notes detail will print project annotation that may explain the reasons for the variance.

Another part of the definition of a Report is the option to sort the project data, which can be found by clicking the Sort tab in this dialog. The user can sort by up to three fields, along with the usual options to sort in ascending or descending order. In Figure 12-7, the Unstarted Tasks report is sorted in Ascending order on the Start field and then by the ID field.

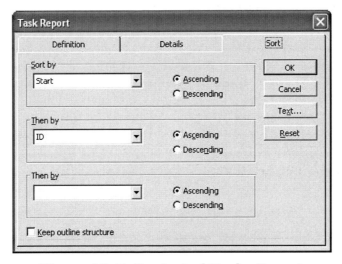

**Figure 12-7: Unstarted Tasks Report
dialog, Sort Page**

The final report detail that you may select is the font to be used in the printing of the report, which can be selected by clicking the Text button on any of the pages of the Unstarted Tasks Report. Because the standard font selected for each Report (Arial regular 8 pt.) may print too small for you to read easily when printed on your default printer, it is often helpful to select a larger font size. For example, the font for all items in the Report is set to Arial regular 10 pt in the Text Styles dialog, as is displayed in Figure 12-8.

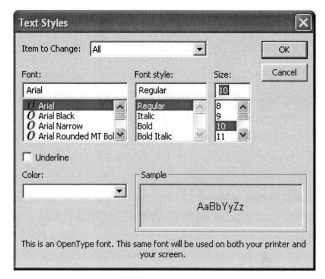

**Figure 12-8: Text Styles dialog**

 You can change the text styles for any type of item in the Report by clicking the Item to change drop-down list and selecting the type of task to change.

 If you find that the default Font settings for any Report prints text that is too small to read easily, msProjectExperts recommends that you make the following settings in the Text Styles dialog:

- Item to change: *All*
- Font: *Arial*
- Font style: *Regular*
- Size: *10*

These new settings will produce a much more readable Report.

# Hands On Exercise

## Exercise 12-1

Create a custom task Report based on the new Table and Filter used in the "_msPE Late Dates >= 5d" View.

1. Open the file called "Project Master12" from your student folder

2. Click View ➤ Reports and then double-click the Custom icon

3. Click New and then click OK to create a new Task report

4. In the Name box type "_msPE Late Dates >= 5d"

5. Select _msPE Date Variance as the Table, and select _msPE Late Dates >= 5d as the Filter for this Report

6. Select the Show Summary Tasks option

7. Click the Details tab and select the Notes option in the Task section

8. Click OK and then click the Preview button

Your _msPE Late Dates >= 5d report should appear as is shown in Figure 12-9.

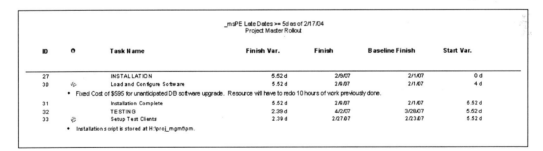

**Figure 12-9: msPE Late Dates >= 5d Report**

9. Close all dialogs, then save but do not close your "Project Master12" file

## *Creating Custom Crosstab Reports*

Microsoft Project 2003 allows you to create four different types of custom Reports: Task, Resource, Monthly Calendar, and Crosstab. The information presented previously in this section is useful for creating both Task and Resource Reports; however, a Crosstab Report is different enough to warrant a separate discussion.

What is a Crosstab Report? The software displays data in a Crosstab report using a grid of columns and rows, with each individual piece of data contained in a cell. In Microsoft Project 2003, a Crosstab report displays task or resource data in a timephased grid, with the time period shown at the top of each column. For example, it is possible to report on the Work performed by each resource in a project on a weekly basis using a Crosstab Report.

To define a Crosstab report in Microsoft Project 2003, it is necessary to select three pieces of data on the Definition page:

- The time periods to be shown in each column of data

- The Field data to be displayed in each row

- A Filter to be used for extracting desired data

Figure 12-10 shows the definition of the Who Does What When report in the Crosstab Report dialog.

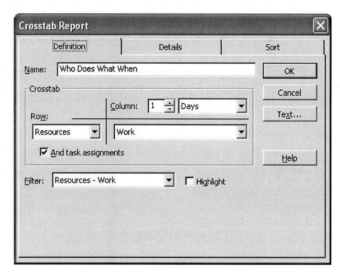

**Figure 12-10: Who Does What When
report, Definition page**

As you can see in Figure 12-10, the Who Does What When Report uses data from the resource Work field in each row. The Report applies the Resources - Work filter to display only Work (not Material) resources. The Report also displays the data on a daily basis in each column.

The details available in the Who Does What When Report include whether to show row and column totals, to display gridlines between tasks and resources, and to repeat the first column of information on every page. Figure 12-11 shows the Details page of the Who Does What When report.

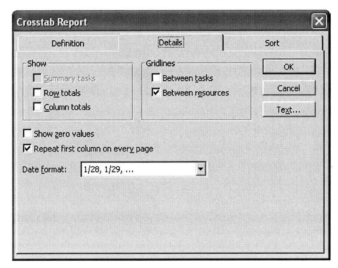

**Figure 12-11: Who Does What When report, Details Page**

 You will probably find that the default Crosstab reports do not report on the time period you desire. For example, the Who Does What When report shows resource work on a daily basis, but you may want to report on a weekly or monthly basis. To create a useful version of this Report, copy it and then modify the copy to your reporting requirements.

# Hands On Exercise

## Exercise 12-2

The project sponsor has requested a custom Report that is similar to the Cash Flow Report, but in which the data is reported on a monthly basis, rather than weekly. Create this new custom Crosstab Report.

1. Click View ➤ Reports and then double-click the Custom icon

2. Select the Cash Flow Report and click the Copy button

3. Name this new Report _msPE Monthly Cash Flow

4. Select Months as the reporting time period in the Column: section

5. Click the OK button, then click the Preview button to Print Preview the new Report

Your new Report should appear as is displayed in Figure 12-12.

_msPE Monthly Cash Flowas of 2/17/04
Project Master Rollout

| | January | February | March | April | May | June | Total |
|---|---|---|---|---|---|---|---|
| Project Master Rollout | | | | | | | |
| Project Status Meeting | | | | | | | |
| INSTALLATION | | | | | | | |
| Order Server | $500.00 | | | | | | $500.00 |
| Setup Server and Load O/S | $2,000.00 | | | | | | $2,000.00 |
| Load and Configure Software | $790.40 | $2,504.61 | | | | | $3,295.01 |
| Installation Complete | | | | | | | |
| TESTING | | | | | | | |
| Setup Test Clients | | $2,500.00 | | | | | $2,500.00 |
| Verify Connectivity | | $162.00 | $1,488.00 | | | | $1,650.00 |
| Troubleshoot Errors | | | $4,666.67 | $133.33 | | | $4,800.00 |
| Testing Complete | | | | | | | |
| TRAINING | | | | | | | |
| Create Training Materials | | | | $5,440.00 | | | $5,440.00 |
| Conduct Skills Assessment | | | | $3,200.00 | | | $3,200.00 |
| Create Training Schedule | | | | $26.67 | $933.33 | | $960.00 |
| Provide PM Theory Training | | | | | $2,240.00 | | $2,240.00 |
| Provide Training | | | | | $8,800.00 | $800.00 | $9,600.00 |
| Project Complete | | | | | | | |
| Total | $5,070.40 | $6,946.61 | $7,934.67 | $11,045.00 | $13,769.33 | $2,596.00 | $47,362.01 |

**Figure 12-12: _msPE Monthly Cash Flow report**

6. Close the Print Preview window

7. Use the Organizer to copy your two new Reports to your Global.mpt file

8. Close all dialogs, then save but *do not* close your "Project Master12" file

# Printing in Microsoft Project 2003

In Microsoft Project 2003, printing can be a challenge, knowing that the software may not print on paper what you see on your screen. Whether printing a Report or a View, the following features of Microsoft Project 2003 will assist you with reporting project information.

## *Print Preview*

The first step to effective printing is to use Print Preview. Doing this step first will save you lots of paper and frustration! To access Print Preview, use either of the following methods:

- Click the File menu, and then click Print Preview
- Click the Print Preview button on the Standard toolbar.

## *Page Setup*

While in Print Preview, you may need to change one or more printing options in the Page Setup dialog. To access the Page Setup dialog, use either of the following methods:

- If you are in the Print Preview window, click the Page Setup button at the top of the window
- If you are not in Print Preview, click the File menu, then click Page Setup

Figure 12-13 shows the Page options page of the Page Setup dialog.

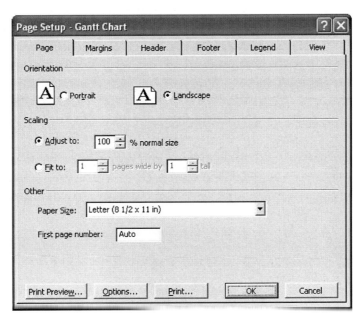

**Figure 12-13: Page Setup dialog**
**Page options**

Tables 12-1 through 12-6 describe the options available on each page of the Page Setup dialog.

| Page options | |
| --- | --- |
| Orientation | Portrait or Landscape |
| Scaling | Adjust to: to reduce or enlarge the printed image<br><br>Fit to: scale the printed view to a certain number of pages |
| Other | Set paper size<br>Set the number of the first page |

**Table 12-1: Page options**

| Margins options | |
| --- | --- |
| Margins | Set margins for top, bottom, left, and right |
| Borders around | Place borders around every page, outer pages only, or no pages |

**Table 12-2: Margins options**

| Header options | |
| --- | --- |
| Preview | Displays a print preview of the completed Header (the preview is not to scale) |
| Alignment | Up to five lines of text, field code or project information can be entered in the Left, Center, and Right header<br><br>All text can be formatted and previewed<br><br>Click buttons to add printing information such as Page Number, Total Number of Pages, Date and Time stamps, File Name, and even clipart |
| General | Add other page information fields |
| Project Fields | Add Row 0 information from project fields |

**Table 12-3: Header options**

You can also access the Header section of the Page Setup dialog by clicking View ➢ Header and Footer.

| Footer options | |
|---|---|
| Preview | Displays a print preview of the completed Footer (the preview is not to scale) |
| Alignment | Up to three lines of text, field code or project information can be entered in the Left, Center, and Right footer<br><br>All text can be formatted and previewed<br><br>Click buttons to add printing information such as Page Number, Total Number of Pages, Date and Time stamps, File Name, and even clipart |
| General | Add other page information fields |
| Project Fields | Add Row 0 information from project fields |

**Table 12-4: Footer options**

 You can also access the Footer section of the Page Setup dialog by clicking View ➢ Header and Footer.

The Legend is found in the bottom of the printed page when printing the Gantt Chart, Network Diagram, or Calendar views. The software prints the default Legend on every page and includes a text section 2 inches wide on the left end where you can include customized information.

| Legend options | |
| --- | --- |
| Preview | Displays a print preview of the completed Legend text (the preview is not to scale) |
| Alignment | Up to three lines of text, field code or project information can be entered in the Left, Center, and Right of the Legend label<br><br>All text can be formatted and previewed<br><br>Click buttons to add printing information such as Page Number, Total Number of Pages, Date and Time stamps, File Name, and even clipart |
| Legend on | Can be printed on every page, a single page, or none |
| Legend Labels | Change the font for the Legend text |

**Table 12-5: Legend options**

| View options | |
| --- | --- |
| Print all sheet columns | Print all columns in the table, regardless of how many are currently visible in the View |
| Print first ___ columns on all pages | Print the selected number of columns on every page |
| Print notes | Notes are printed on a separate page at the end of the printout |
| Print blank pages | Prints blank pages in large Network Diagram view |
| Fit timescale to end of page | Fits the timescale through available space |

**Table 12-6: View options**

 When you are in an assignment view, such as Task Usage or Resource Usage, you have two additional options available that allow the printing of row and column totals.

 The *Print first ___ columns on all pages* option guarantees that the software will print the selected number of columns on every page, regardless of the number of columns presently visible in the View. However, if additional columns are entirely visible in the View, the software will print them, but only on the first page.

 You cannot access the Legend and View pages of the Page Setup dialog when preparing to print a Report. They are only visible when preparing to print a View.

## *Using the Print Dialog*

Once you have successfully selected your options in the Page Setup dialog, you are ready to print. To print, use either of the following methods, which will display the Print dialog:

- Click the Print button while in Print Preview
- Click File ➢ Print

Figure 12-14 shows the Print dialog.

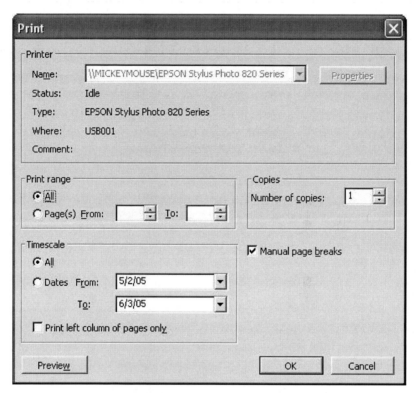

**Figure 12-14: Print dialog**

Table 12-7 describes important options in the Print dialog.

| Option | Description |
|---|---|
| Timescale | Specifies the timescale range within which you want to print |
| Print left column of pages only | Prints only the leftmost pages of a view, even though tasks might span more than one page |
| Manual Page Breaks | Place a check in the box to print using manually inserted page breaks<br><br>With the checkbox cleared, the automatic page breaks will be used, regardless of inserted manual page breaks |

**Table 12-7: Print options**

## Hands On Exercise

### Exercise 12-3

Use the Page Setup options to print a View.

1. Apply the Gantt Chart view, if necessary
2. Pull the vertical split bar slightly to the left to cover up part (but not all) of the Duration column
3. Click the Print Preview button on the Standard toolbar

Notice that the Duration column is not displayed in the Print Preview window. This is because the column is partially hidden.

4. Click the Page Setup button and then select the View tab in the Page Setup dialog
5. Select the Print first __ columns on all pages option and then set the spin control to 4 columns
6. Click the Print Preview button

Notice that the Duration column is now displayed in the Print Preview window because of the option setting we just selected.

7. Click the Close button to close the Print Preview window

### Exercise 12-4

Print a selected date range for a View.

1. Apply the Resource Usage view
2. Click the Print Preview button on the Standard toolbar
3. Click the Print button at the top of the window
4. In the Timescale section of the Print dialog, select a date range from 1/1/07 to 1/31/07 only
5. Click the Preview button

Notice that the Print Preview window displays only that portion of the timephased grid between our selected dates, plus a few extra days to fill out the rest of the final page.

6. Save and close your "Project Master12" project file

# An Issue with Printing Views

One of the problems that you may face when printing a View is that Microsoft Project 2003 prints only those columns that are *completely visible* in the Task Sheet. We addressed this issue in Exercise 12-3. For example, notice in Figure 12-15 that the vertical split bar is covering part of the contents of the Duration column.

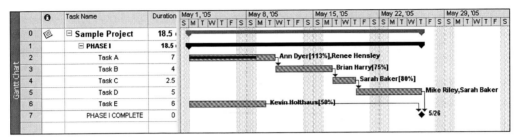

**Figure 12-15: Duration column
partially hidden**

When attempting to print this View, Microsoft Project 2003 will not print the Duration column because it is not completely visible. To guarantee that the software will print the desired number of columns, set the *Print first ___ columns on all pages* option to 4 columns. When determining the number of columns to be printed, remember to count the ID number column.

# msProjectExperts

# EPM Learning

*Other Titles available*

- ## For Administrators:

    ***Administering an Enterprise PMO Using Microsoft Office Project Server 2003*** • ISBN 0-9759828-1-8

- ## For Project Managers:

    ***Managing Enterprise Projects using Microsoft Office Project Server 2003*** • ISBN 0-9759828-0-X

- ## For Resource Managers:

    ***Managing Enterprise Resources using Microsoft Office Project Server 2003*** • ISBN 0-9759828-2-6

- ## For Team Members:

    ***Collaborating on Enterprise Project Teams using Microsoft Office Project Server 2003*** • ISBN 0-9759828-3-4

- ## For Executive Management:

    ***Mining Your EPM Portfolio using Microsoft Office Project Server 2003*** • ISBN 0-9759828-4-2

- ## For Advanced Project Users:

    ***Mastering Advanced Project Management using Microsoft Office Project 2003*** • ISBN 0-9759828-6-9

www.msprojectexperts.com • 908-626-1404